THE COIN FROM CALABRIA

Discovering the Historical Roots of My Calabrian People.

Michael Caputo

Michael Caputo

ISBN-13:978-1484907665
ISBN-10:1484907663

To my children, Anthony, Julie and Victor and all the descendents of Calabria around the world.

TABLE OF CONTENTS

ACKNOWLEDGMENTS

Some time ago, I called Dr. Giuseppe Greco, an expert on ancient Calabrian history, to thank him for his labor of love in uncovering so many wonderful details about our ancient past. Dr. Greco, in his inimitable, humble way, replied that his work was built on the shoulders of giants. In time, I realized that he was being truthful. We owe much to many ancient historians, and, especially, to Calabrian historians, such as Barrio, Marafioti, Fiore, etc., who, centuries ago, wrote detailed histories of our Calabrian people. We also owe much to academics of our days that focused specifically on the history of the Angitola Valley. Among such, I want to first of all offer my deepest gratitude to the above-mentioned, venerable Dr. Giuseppe Greco, from Maierato, whom I had the pleasure of visiting in the Summer of 2010. Though he was battling the results of a serious paralysis, due to a stroke, his mind was impressively sharp and his ability to recall details from ancient works was nothing short of astounding. I also want to thank archeologist, Cristiana La Serra, who has written an impressive thesis on the Rocca Angitola, and other nearby locations. In my view, she is well on her way to becoming the foremost expert on the history and the archeology of the Angitola Valley. Her father, my relative and friend, Pino La Serra, has provided me with information, maps and books that have proven invaluable in my search. He is the kind of friend we all should have. My deepest gratitude to Giuseppe Maio, from Monterosso Calabro, who has kindly contributed the very beautiful pictures that enrich the section on La Rocca Angitola. Thanks also go to my teacher-daughter, Julie Caputo, and my wife, Leonilda for their helpful suggestions. There are many others whose works have been quoted that space does not allow me to mention. Their works will receive due acknowledgement in the Works Cited section. Lastly, I want to thank my wife and children who patiently bore my obsessive pursuit of this new project. Thank you, Leonilda, Anthony, Julie and Victor. You are greatly loved.
Michael Caputo

Michael Caputo

PREFACE

I am starting this book on December 31, 2009, around 5 PM, in a suburb of a North American city. The New Year is fast approaching. Soon some family members will come to have dinner with my family. Before the evening begins, I would like to finally start something that is near to my heart: a book about the search for the origins of an ancient coin I found as a child, which, in time, led me into a much more exciting adventure: to the search for the ancient origins of my people.

I have asked myself why I would want to write and publish such a work, and I have concluded that there are three fundamental reasons.

First of all, I would like my children to know, in detail, and in depth, stories that I shared with them several times, but never did in a complete, and orderly way. It would also be a wonderful opportunity to teach them about their ancestors on their father's side.

I also want to help the great many who share the same genetic, and historic roots to get to know their enthralling ancient past.

Lastly, I would like this book to become a source of inspiration for all who crave to know more about their ancient roots. As I will show in this book, patience, determination, and a systematic approach can lead to uncovering surprising, and amazing facts about one's ancestors; facts that now, more than ever, can be uncovered with the help of rich libraries and the Internet.

I hope my labor will prove to be enlightening to my children, and all of those with whom I am genetically related. I equally hope that all who will read this book will be inspired to dig further through the various historical layers to uncover the wonders of *their* past.

INTRODUCTION

Many years have gone by, since the events you will read about in this book took place in a far away location. I lived in that location as a child until age fourteen, when I left with my parents for another country where I have been given many wonderful opportunities.

Life has been good to me in Canada where I have lived for decades, and where I have raised a special family. But, often, my thoughts fly back to a little town, in a country far away, where some of my happiest years were spent, and where I experienced some of my most unforgettable moments.

One experience hangs in the most central part of my mind. It started on a hot Summer's day, and it gave rise to a chapter in my life that keeps on being written to this day.

1. A BOY IN CALABRIA

The story begins in 1963, or 1964. I was either ten, or eleven. It was another very hot, and uneventful Summer's day in the town of Capistrano, in the last southern Region of Italy named Calabria. I probably had made my usual morning tour of the piazza nearby; I had strolled north and south on the main road, the Via Nazionale; I stood on the edge of the Via, by the waist-high wall that kept us kids from falling into the steep ravine below; I looked down the meandering valley, and then raised my eyes toward the Rocca Angitola Mountain, and the blue Mediterranean, far in the distance, as I had done a thousand times before. I paused to inspect the digging that had gone on for weeks in the ravine below where the eager workers were clearing the area for the high pillars that would have held up the Mayor's house, so as to bring it to road level.

It was just another boring day, with little to do but wait until one of us kids in my area would have thought of something to do to add some fun to the monotony of another hot Summer' day. Then the boredom suddenly ended…

"LOOK WHAT I FOUND!"

I remember being in front of my house, near Four Corners, where the town's two major streets intersect, when one of my young friends approached me, all excited. Was it Raffaele, or

Modesto, or maybe Mimmo? I don't recall. I do recall, though, that one of them came to announce a dramatic, life-changing event. He had just found some old-looking coins in the ravine where the Mayor's house was to be built.

My friend looked elated, as he recounted the visit down the steep ravine, and his amazing find. Filled with childhood curiosity, he had gone to simply look around and, upon glancing at the moist, dark dirt he saw an old-looking coin. He stooped down, looked attentively, and then collected it with excitement. But there were more–several more. He continued looking and finding, for quite some time. When there were no more to be found, he ran hastily to share the amazing news with his closest friends–and I was one of his lucky friends.

It was not a kids' trick meant to break the day's monotony; the evidence was there, in his trembling hands. Sure they were dirty, and very old looking, but they were real, and they looked like nothing we had ever seen before. A close scrutiny revealed that most were old, Italian coins.

I stared at the coins, mesmerized. I had never seen such amazing, old coins before. To my delight, my friend let go of them one by one, to let me touch them, to read the names, and the dates as evidence that he, indeed, was the proud possessor of an amazing treasure.

Within minutes, the group grew, and so did the excitement. We all agreed that the ravine must have had more coins waiting to be found and, as we had done so many times before, we went on to tackle our newest adventure.

The ravine was nearby. The fastest way to get to the bottom was the stone, and concrete stairs beside my house. We ran quickly down the steps, and reached the promising area within seconds, ready to search, and find more coins.

All of us looked around with eager eyes, and soon found what we were looking for. In spite of all the coins already found by our friend, the dirt offered us plenty more.

We searched for a long time and, to our delight, we found many more. Each time our eyes landed on another coin, we proudly yelled, "I FOUND ANOTHER ONE!!" for all to hear. Soon our pockets were full, and our young hearts were filled with gladness.

Then the coins became rare and, when it became clear that we could not find any more, we left satisfied. We then walked to the nearby fountain to wash the bounty thoroughly, and to check the dates.

By late afternoon, the unavoidable competition began. Who had found the most coins? Who had the *oldest* coin? Unfortunately, as I recall, that honor was not mine, though I did have in my possession several old coins.

We went back the next day, and maybe the day after. A few more coins were found but, in time, the coins dried up and, since digging was too time consuming for our impatient group, the search came to an end–*except for me.*

You see, I was the lucky one; I lived right next to the ravine.

In fact my bedroom faced the very spot where the coins had been found–*and I was very persistent.*

PERSEVERANCE PAID OFF

My ten-year-old logic told me that more coins were waiting to be found. So I conceived a system that was quite ingenious for a ten year old. I would dig a hole around half a foot deep; I would then create a small vertical wall on one side of the hole, and I would slowly scrape the dirt off the wall with a small twig. It would have taken time, and much patience–but I was in for the challenge.

Being totally alone, I could focus on each grain of dirt, and each pebble. I treated the miniature wall with the respect one owes to any fragile object, and dug *slowly* and *gently*.

The dark, moist dirt scraped off easily. I inspected closely anything that looked like a clump of dirt. I knew that the dirt would have built up around anything hard; especially metal coins.

Dirt, stones, twigs and other parts of indefinable objects had been deposited in that location over a great many years, layer after layer, by the flood of water that would gather during rainstorms from the upper part of town and pour into the ravine.

I continued looking at everything I found closely, and with intensity. The search went on for awhile–and then it happened…

I felt the twig touch something hard. I looked closely. Was it just another pebble, a clump of hard dirt, or was it something else? I pushed the twig gently behind the promising clump, and pushed it out of the surrounding dirt. I then picked it up and inspected it closely.

At first glance, it looked like a dirt-encrusted button; but it felt heavier than a button. I rubbed my fingers against both surfaces, but the crust was very hard, and would not come off.

I was so intrigued by my find that I stopped the dig. I rushed up the steps on the side of the ravine, and walked hastily toward the nearby fountain. I washed, and scrubbed, and washed some more. Gradually, the hardened dirt wore off, and my hopes were validated. It was not a button–it was another coin.

The irregular circle framed what looked like an ancient face, like the ones I had seen in history books. On the other side appeared what looked like a horn-like shape. It was clearly a very old coin; without doubt, older than all the ones that had already been found.

Proud of my discovery, I rushed to show it to my friends. I had suddenly become the undisputed winner of the coin war, and I wanted all to know. They, one by one, looked at my coin with tangible envy. This time, victory was mine. Given the amazing find, we probably went back for more, but the search may have been in vain. I do not recall sharing my technique with anyone. I probably guarded it jealousy for future use.

I returned another time and continued the search, but, finally, even my technique failed to produce more fruit. Happy with my find, I rested on my laurels.

Not long after, holes were dug deep into the ravine's dark

ground, and, soon after, the workers poured cement into them. Afterwards, tall, wooden casings were nailed together and concrete pillars rose to road level. Soon the first floor was shaped, and the location became inaccessible. Finally, the search for ancient coins was officially over.

In the few days that followed, the excitement of the finds gradually waned. The time had come for another adventure. Someone suggested searching for old stamps. We all found it to be a great idea, and another adventure began which lasted for several months.

Capistrano: A shimmering town surrounded by olive groves in the southern Italian Region of Calabria.

Four Corners, and Via Nazionale. The tall house on the left is the former Mayor's house. The coin was found where its foundations now rest.

UNCOVERING THE TRUTH

The coin was still covered with a brown film that would not wash off. Its total beauty, and specific age were yet to be uncovered. But soap and water was simply not enough. Something more powerful had to be found.

One day, my parents went to visit the city of Vibo Valentia, the largest city in our area. My father and mother went to shop at a store on the main street. I noticed, nearby, a hardware store. I told my parents I would have gone next door to buy something, and they allowed me to go. I quickly went to the hardware store, walked to the back, and asked a man behind a counter if he had anything strong enough to clean metals. He did.

He looked on the shelf behind him, and found a small bottle. I bought the promising bottle which contained a milky substance. I was eager to go home to try the miracle liquid, to see what else was hiding behind the dark, brown film which still covered my precious coin.

Once home, I immediately poured a few drops of the promising white, thick substance on one side of the coin, and quickly wiped it off with a white cloth. A black stain appeared on the cloth while, simultaneously, a clearly formed head of a woman emerged.

I turned the coin to the other side, and repeated the process. The horn suddenly became more pronounced, and something unclear appeared, as if coming out from it. It wasn't just a horn–it was a "Cornucopia," otherwise known as a "Horn of Plenty." I do not recall if I repeated the process more than once. I do remember being concerned that such a potent substance could have eaten into the coin, and could have damaged it; so I stopped using it.

There was no doubt about it: the head was that of someone ancient; perhaps someone from ancient Rome. At that point, I knew for sure that I had a real winner, but, unfortunately, I could not see any date. The only thing I could see was what looked like a "5" or an "S" on both sides.

More proud than ever, I put the coins in a small metal box and I hid them in a well-protected location; then back I went to my stamp collecting. That unforgettable Summer finally came to an end, and we all went back to school.

Both sides of the ancient coin.

ALMOST ROBBED OF MY TREASURE

One day, probably not long after school started, I brought my ancient coin to school. I had shown it off to my fellow students; I believe, I also wanted to show my teachers how special I had become.

That morning I told a male teacher about the coin, and he immediately asked to see it. As expected, he too was mesmerized by it. He looked at both sides intently, and repeatedly, and then he went on to pronounce himself as to its identity: "This coin is a Roman coin," he told me with confidence; "This is a Roman Sextersius."

I heard the magical words pour out from his lips, and I quickly stored them in my mind, so as to never forget them. Finally, I had the pronouncement of an Authority; finally, I knew for sure it was a *very old,* "Roman" coin, and that it was a, "Sextersius."

But the Authority did not stop at simply informing me about my coin. After sharing his precious knowledge with me, he paused for an instant and, with a wily smile, he invitingly said: "Why don't you give it to me?"

I may have been only ten, or eleven, but I was not the kind of kid who would separate himself from his treasure, simply to ingratiate himself with a teacher. I knew, instantly, what he was up to, and refused to go along with his game.

"No!" I said firmly, with a pleasant, but *fake* smile. That was *my* coin and no one was going to take it away from me–and that included the one who had finally given it an identity.

The teacher did not insist. He knew when a "no" was a definite "no," and I made it very clear that my "no!" was very definite.

From that day on, I never again brought my coin to school and, never again, as far as I can recall, did I show it to anyone else in my town.

I believe that not long after my cousin Domenico Caputo and his family left for Toronto, Canada. He and I and a crew of about twenty others had been in the same class since kindergarten. For the five years of elementary school we had been privileged to have been taught by the firm and caring, Maestro Giuseppe Fera, and we had been again in the same class for two years in junior high. I was convinced that he, like a few other friends who had left before him, would have disappeared for many years before I would have seen him again, but I was pleasantly proven wrong just a few years later.

THE COIN'S ORIGINAL OWNER

The school year ended. The ravine where the coin had been found had nothing else to offer. The Mayor's house had risen to its two intended floors, and had robbed me of my balcony's view of the Rocca Mountain and the Mediterranean. The land of treasures was no more.

Another Summer began and, like all other summers, we kids tried our best to keep busy. We played soccer on the uneven, dirt road near the cemetery; we gathered together to hear young and musically gifted, Raffaele, play his accordion; we walked around town, and did our best not to be bored.

Around this time my sister, Grazia gave birth to my nephew, Saverio, followed by Tony around a year later. It was a joyful time.

Also, during this time, my mother, or a family friend, told me that many years before a monk, who had lived not very far from my house, had owned a large collection of ancient coins. The coins we found may have been part of the monk's collection.

If this was true, it is quite possible that after his death his relatives may have found the collection, saw no value in the old and "useless" coins and, to our future delight, they threw them away in the nearby ravine. I cannot conceive of the monk doing so himself since, as I found out later, he was a cultured and knowledgeable man. The collection must have been dear to him until his death. If anyone threw them away, it must have been relatives who had no idea of the unpardonable sin they were committing, by tossing away such a treasure. Thankfully, decades later, we children found, and saved most of the precious coins from oblivion. I don't know where my friends' coins ended up, but I can assure the reader that my coins, to this day, are very well protected.

Coins of the Vatican, and King Victor Emanuel III. These coins were also found during my search.

The fountain in Four Corners (bottom, left): The location where the washing of the dirty, old coins took place.

2. RENOIR IN CAPISTRANO?

The new school year began. New teachers appeared. My new art teacher, Franco Natale, was wonderful to have. He was brimming with energy; he was confident, creative, and always warm and friendly. He belonged to the Natale family, a family of very gifted people, artistically and musically. His grandfather was Maestro Natale, who many years ago had been the town's Postmaster, the town's Mayor, and the Maestro of the local band. My father, who knew him well, described him as eccentric, intense, and brilliant. His genes clearly were passed on to some of his descendents who later excelled in various fields.

Franco was particularly gifted in art. He had discovered his artistic talents, while in the police force. Later, he became an art teacher, and I had the privilege of being one of his students. Little did we know that the tall, dynamic, and enthusiastic man, many years later would have become a very successful, award-winning artist.

One day, Mr. Natale shared with us something which, by the look on his face, appeared to be particularly important. He announced to us grade sevens something he had concluded about *The Baptism of Jesus* mural found on the wall behind the baptistery of our main church. His conclusion was that it had been painted by a man whose name we had never heard before: "Renoir."

We had no idea of who Renoir had been, but we knew that he

had to have been an important painter. It was also evident by the name that he was not Italian.

Mr. Natale announced that he was planning to ask the people from the government department who dealt with art to come and look at the mural, so as to validate his views. I stored the announcement in the same location of my mind where the name of my coin had been stored, so as not to be forgotten–and it was never forgotten.

Probably the Summer that followed, while I was playing in the piazza, I saw Mr. Natale, Don Nicolino Manfrida, our parish priest, and two authoritative-looking people enter the church. I was quite sure Mr. Natale was showing them the mural. I do not recall how long they stayed in the church, but I immediately suspected that they had to have been the people Mr. Natale was hoping to get to come and investigate. Of course, I had no way of validating my suspicion and, to this today, I have no idea as to who they were.

I heard nothing about their verdict. But I did not forget the evolving story. I kept all the details stored in my mind. The verdict was finally rendered several years later.

Upon my return home, many years later, I found that according to some authorities Mr. Natale's views had been validated. According to them, Renoir, the famed French impressionist painter, had indeed come to our town, and he had restored parts, or all of the mural, as his son had written about in his biography, *Renoir my Father.*

I have recently discovered that, in reality, Mr. Natale had not been the first one to conclude that Renoir had visited, and had done some work in my town. Two teachers, who were teaching in Capistrano, and a journalist from a nearby city had reached this conclusion before Mr. Natale, after reading Renoir's biography. Mr. Natale was informed of the possibility by his two colleagues and he, too, quickly became a firm supporter of that point of view.

In the French artist's biography, Renoir's son describes his father's trip to Calabria, intended to visit a priest, whom he had met while in Naples. The priest described to him the beauty of Calabria, and that inspired Renoir to travel south to visit the area. "While in Naples, Renoir stayed in a little inn patronized especially by the clergy. 'When we sat down to eat spaghetti with tomato sauce, I was the only not dressed in black.'"[i]

He then shares that his father, "...had great discussions on theology with a man next to him, a gaunt priest with a huge nose." He continues, "The priest in question was from Calabria and his description of his part of the country gave my father a desire to see it. And so Renoir set out with a letter of introduction from the Bishop, which his friend had obtained."[ii]

Because there were few railroads, and roads in Calabria, "...he did part of the journey in a fishing boat, going from one port to another and the rest on foot." The French painter used the bishop's letter to help him find accommodations in priests' homes along the way, who showed him much kindness. "Often a parish priest who had only a pallet to sleep on would turn it over to him, and go himself to sleep in the stable with the donkey."[iii]

What left Renoir surprised about Calabria was the abject poverty of the area. Yet, in spite of their poor condition, Calabrians welcomed Renoir warmly, and did their best to make his visit as comfortable as possible. "The poverty of the region was almost unbelievable. Yet everyone put himself out to receive the visitor."[iv]

The food eaten by our ancestors consisted of a few basics. "The meals were more than simple. In some villages the inhabitants lived entirely on beans, and had seldom tasted spaghetti or macaroni..."[v]

Because of lack of bridges, Renoir had difficulty crossing some rivers swollen by heavy rains. In one case, he told his son, that he had no way of crossing one particular river. The solution was offered by a peasant woman who saw him unable to cross. She called a dozen or so other peasants who were working in the fields nearby, and "...they all came to the rescue, laughing and chattering in their dialect..." The peasants came up with an ingenious solution: "They picked up my father and his baggage, waded into the river, and forming a line across it, passed him from one to another like a rugby football."[vi]

Renoir was so touched by their kindness that he offered to reciprocate, but they were not particularly interested in his money, and gladly accepted a portrait of their "bambino" instead.[vii]

Renoir's son then shares the most relevant detail: "In a mountain village Renoir restored the frescoes, which had been destroyed by humidity." Renoir told his son that he had no experience in fresco painting, nor did have the necessary paints to do the job. Being resourceful, he found what he needed at a local mason's. "I didn't know much about fresco painting. I found some paints in powder form, at the mason's in the village." Given the low quality of the material used, he later asked himself, "I wonder if what I did lasted."[viii]

Pierre Auguste Renoir: Considered one of the greatest masters of the Impressionist period in art.

His stay in Calabria, and my village, must have been exceptionally positive. His final assessment of my people gives me a deep feeling of sadness mixed with pride. "All the Calabrians I met were generous and so cheerful in the midst of their poverty."[ix] Though Calabrians in those challenging days lived in poverty, they coped with the paucity in their lives with cheerfulness, and were very kind, and giving people toward strangers.

According to Pino La Serra, a local artist, and President of the

Renoir in Capistrano Association, Renoir went to my town and, upon visiting the local church in the company of Don Francesco Bongiorno, the town's wealthiest man, he saw behind the baptistery a mural badly damaged by humidity. Renoir was shocked by the condition of the fresco. Don Francesco asked him if he could repair it. After at first refusing, he promised him that, upon his return from his trip to other southern areas, he would have fulfilled his wishes.

Renoir kept his word, in May of 1882, when he returned to Capistrano, and completed the promised work in the space of three days.

Among other proofs, a drawing titled, *Calabrian Landscape,* by Renoir, is offered by Pino as further evidence that Renoir had, indeed, come and worked in my town. The drawing shows Capistrano as it looked in the late 1800's, as seen from the Batia area, with our church clearly represented in the distance.[x]

In recent years, more evidence of Renoir's visit to Capistrano, and of his work on the "Baptism of Jesus," and other murals has been offered by the local artist-philosopher, Mario Guarna, in his book, *Gli affreschi di Renoir a Capistrano* (*Renoir's Frescos in Capistrano*). In his book, Mario proposes interesting stylistic evidence to support the presence of Renoir's touch in some of the frescos found in the church.

More recently, local journalist and writer, Andrea Fera, has also joined forces with the other competent minds, with his book, *Renoir in Calabria*, which also offers evidence that, indeed, Renoir came to Capistrano, and did retouch some murals in our church.[xixii]

The fact that Renoir came to Capistrano, and that he left his artistic witness in the main church became a source of great pride for my people who had, up to that point, so little to be proud of. The square where I spent so many special moments as a child was renamed, "Piazza Renoir." Presently tourists that tour our area of Calabria are, on occasion, taken to see the Capistrano Renoir, to the delight of many Capistranesi.

The Baptism of Jesus: Mural restored by Renoir while in Capistrano. *(M. Caputo)*

Renoir may have also restored the frescos behind the church's main altar (top center). (M. Caputo)

Pino La Serra: Artist, and President of the Renoir in Capistrano Association. He has contributed invaluable research which has helped confirm that Renoir visited Capistrano in the late 1800's. He has also provided me with very helpful historical material for this work.

Piazza Renoir: Named after the famed French artist.

THE YEARLY MADONNA CELEBRATIONS

The coin and stamp collecting phase may have come to an end, but we children were soon to enter the most exciting time of year: the Madonna celebrations, which took place the second Sunday in August. This was a day that all Capistranesi, young and old, longed for every year. The special celebration is known to Capistranesi as, "La Festa della Madonna della Montagna,"(The Feast of the Madonna of the Mountain).

This was a yearly event meant to honor Mary, the mother of Jesus, and her statue found on the central altar of the main church. The statue is dressed in a stunning, shining, light-yellow, flowing dress, and a blue mantle, both of which, without doubt, are made of high-quality cloth.

The crowned Mary sits with a regal posture inside the glass niche illuminated by soft, cool lights. Her face is pink, youthful, and loving. Her baby Jesus stands erect on Mary's left leg, clothed with a shimmering, somewhat feminine, yellow, baby dress, but with a confident, divine demeanor.

Most Italian towns worship Mary, but with slight variations. They are all given a somewhat different name; they have a somewhat different look; their dress is also somewhat different. Yet, they all have the same reassuring, and loving, motherly appearance.

My town's Madonna was, "Mary of the Mountain." To the people of my town she was, and remains special above all others. She also was the ultimate source of comfort, and all took time to visit her in the church whenever possible, to bathe in her warmth, and in her love.

Of course, no one gave much importance to the fact that Mary had, in actuality, been imported from another Calabrian town and, thus, her other name: "La Madonna di Polsi," (The Madonna from Polsi); Polsi being the name of the town she had been worshipped in, long before she started being worshipped in our town.

In the 1700's, a priest by the name of Don Domenico Zerbi was assigned to serve in Capistrano. In July of 1757, he went to Polsi on a pilgrimage, and brought back to Capistrano various icons of the Madonna, which were placed in the local church for worship. In time, a statue was commissioned. The sculptor who took on the job was maestro Antonio Reggio, who came down from Naples to accomplish the task. The statue was finally delivered, and was consecrated the Sunday after Easter, in 1759.

Since then the statue has become the most beloved, sacred object in our town. The image remains chiseled in the hearts of Capistranesi around the world who have retained their Catholic faith. Most of them return home, when possible, to see their families, and their special mother, during the time of the "Festa della Madonna della Montagna," which takes place on the second Sunday in August.

The attachment to this statue is so strong that the two biggest Capistrano communities abroad have each commissioned a replica of their beloved Madonna, so as to celebrate her on the second Sunday of August, as they did back home.

But, not very long ago, the story has taken an unexpected twist. A few Capistranesi in the Australian community who read Jehovah's Witnesses' material, concluded that one of the Commandments forbids the worship of statues and pictures. As a result, they stopped participating in the Madonna's celebrations, and then went on to share their beliefs with others in the community who also embraced their ideas. The number of Capistranesi who left Catholicism apparently became so large that the Melbourne celebrations stopped altogether.

In the future, will the same fate assail the Toronto community, and their Madonna celebrations? Time will tell.

3. GOING TO "AMERICA!"

In June, 1967, as I was playing in the foyer of the Palazzo Brizzi, where the middle school was being hosted, my father suddenly, and furtively, appeared in the entrance, and asked me to follow him.

I was confused; it was about midday, school was not yet over, and my father had come to school to take me home. He had never done this before, and the whole thing was puzzling. I tried to get an explanation, but he walked hastily in front of me, and was very evasive. "Be quiet, and just follow me!" he said firmly.

We walked hastily down the Corso; we crossed the empty square, and within a few minutes we were home. Then the news: the time had come to leave for Canada.

The big cardboard suitcases were ready. My few clothes had been packed. I quickly made sure my coins were safely stowed away. We would have been driven to the Saint Eufemia train station on a 60's Fiat minivan.

The neighbors were informed at the last minute, and the news spread like wildfire. Antonio, the barber, Teresa, and Michele were leaving for America. A large group of people gathered around us to give us their emotional goodbyes. I promised my best friend I would have written; I told the others I would have returned. Then off we went, and on to my newest adventure—one that would have never left me bored again.

THE AMAZING TRIP BEGINS

I looked behind me, as the car was leaving my beloved town. I waved goodbye to my friends, from the back seat of the car. We slowly drove north, leaving behind the centre of town where my house was located. I glanced at the meandering valley on my left, the Rocca Mountain, and the Mediterranean Sea. We passed the Maestro Fera's home, the ever-running Batia Fountain, my Nonna's house, and then the last house…

The twisty road took us to Monterosso, the nearby town. We wound our way through the busy streets and, as we were leaving the town, from the back window I saw Brunina, a gracious young lady, and school friend from my town, walking down Monterosso's main street with her mother. She was the last friend I saw that day. She did not see me, and I wish she had, as she was a dear childhood friend. I knew it would have been a very long time until I would have seen her again.

Capistrano's Four Corners. The emotional goodbyes took place in this location.

We traveled down the valley; passed Monterosso's cemetery, and on toward the Angitola Lake. We rode beside the recently-created, artificial lake, and then passed beside the Rocca Angitola Mountain, on our left. I looked up the steep mountain, for the last time. We quickly traveled down to the St. Eufemia Plain, adjacent to the Mediterranean Sea where, within minutes, we reached the area's main train station.

The train trip is a blur. I do not recall how long it took us to get to Naples, or any details surrounding the trip. Most of it must have been a night trip.

My next memories are of the harbor building in the port city of Naples. Its main hall was crowded with old, wooden benches, and hundreds of people waiting to board the gigantic ship nearby. Not far from the port, I do remember seeing an impressive castle with very high walls, and the lofty Vesuvius in the distance. Then the unforgettable trip began.

We boarded the Cristoforo Colombo liner, one of the major passenger ships in the Italian fleet. It was huge, and swift, and it would have taken us to our destination in about nine days. The ship was filled with Italian and Greek emigrants, and many American and Canadian tourists who were returning home from their trip to "Romantic Italy."

I can never forget the ship's gradual departure; the hand waving from the pier; the picturesque harbor, the majestic Vesuvius, and the gradual disappearance of the city of Naples. As Italy was disappearing on the horizon, I must have felt deep sadness mixed with a longing for the promising and exciting unknown.

My family was assigned to a round dining table for the whole trip. We shared the table with a lovely Italian-Canadian woman, and her two children: a pretty short-haired girl about my age, and her lively younger brother. They had gone to visit family back home, while the dad had stayed back in Canada to work.

The trip was pleasant and exciting, for as long as we were traveling over the placid Mediterranean. The ship was filled with beautiful halls; the lounging areas were spacious and comfortable. Movies in English were being shown in the evening for the English-speaking tourists. I heard the tourists laugh a lot, but I was not interested. Most of my time was spent with the young fellow I ate with, or simply looking at the deep-blue sea stretching out into the endless horizon.

Within two days, the majestic cliffs of Gibraltar appeared on the horizon. I stared at all the visible details of the steep, stony mountain, storing the wonder in my mind to this very day.

About two days after passing by Gibraltar, I was again mesmerized by two Azores islands we passed between. The one on the north side was covered with gloomy clouds, and looked rugged, dark and mysterious; the one facing it, on the south side, looked like an enchanted isle from a fable book, with countless terraced gardens climbing up a mountain, spotted by sparkling white houses and churches. Then, more ocean…

After the Azores, the trip felt long and tiring. Ahead were four more days of gray-blue waters, and cloudy skies. It was during this phase that nausea set in, and it prevented me from even looking at the water. I was forced to spend my time inside the ship, which I gladly did, so as not to feel nauseous.

I shared the cabin with an Italian emigrant who was also going to Canada. The man was quiet and strangely aloof. He asked little of me, and I reciprocated gladly.

After the four dreary, tiring days…finally land!

Before entering the Halifax Harbor, we passed by many small, rocky islands covered with evergreens. The ship moved slowly, as it approached the harbor.

Finally, we reached our longed-for destination.

FROM HALIFAX TO MONTREAL

The ship finally stopped near the pier. We left the ship, tired and hopeful, and finally rested our feet on the land called Canada. The location was the now-famous, "Pier 21." We were then directed to a very large building nearby.

Once inside the building, I saw the Customs' officials on my left, as they were opening the packed, large trunks the immigrants were bringing along. We saw clothes, salamis, and plastic jugs of olive oil being taken out. We heard the uniformed officials trying to communicate with the newcomers. There were questions asked, and justifications offered, but neither side really understood. Some food may have been kept; most was probably mercifully allowed to go on. I was a noisy and chaotic sight.

Afterwards, we entered a large hall with a very high ceiling. The floor was lined with wooden benches, as in Naples, but the hall was larger, and it allowed more space between them. We sat on the first set of benches, as my father tried to sort out where we would get our luggage.

We had no food, and the trip to Montreal would have been a long one. We went to a small convenience store, beside the huge waiting hall and, at the bottom of a shelf, we found some strange-looking bread in plastic bags. It was white, square, and it was cut into many slices. By pressing the bag, one could tell that it was also *very* soft. My parents were puzzled by the staple and giggled. I was intrigued. Little did we know how much of that strange-looking bread we would have eaten in the future.

Because there was no other kind of bread, my father bought it anyway. He also bought either sliced meat or cheese, and we were ready for the next part of our journey.

Pier 21, Halifax, Nova Scotia. A great many Calabrian immigrants landed behind this building, from the 50's to the early 70's. (Skeezix1000)

While in the hall, something happened that I will never forget. As we were sitting on the benches, a beautiful, tall lady, probably in her forties, dressed in a dark-blue uniform, slowly approached me, took what I vaguely remember to have been a lollypop out of a small basket, and gave it to me. Her face exuded warmth and kindness, and made me feel very welcome. The lady, in a way, was symbolic of the nation that would have become my adoptive mother–and I felt reassured. Her memory is chiseled in my heart.

The trip on the old, and decrepit train was far from comfortable. The night came quickly, and so did the cold. It was June, and yet the night air was strangely cold like our month of March. Late at night, a uniformed, older man walked by, and my father stopped him, and acted as though he was shivering. The man understood, smiled, and went to turn on the heating. The rest of the night was comfortable, and restful. He was also a kind-looking human being.

We traveled the whole night, and part of the next day. The train was slow, and stopped several times. The trip must have taken 24 hours, as we reached Montreal late the next evening.

FINALLY IN MONTREAL

Once in the main station in Montreal, we left the train all excited about the nearing reunion with family members I had never met before. I would also soon see again my beloved aunt Maria, Zio Saro, and my dear cousins Rocco, Palma, Mary and Michelina, I had seen depart for Canada a few years before, and Tony and

Alba, born to my aunt while in Canada. We took the escalator and rode on it to the main floor. There we met my uncle Domenic, and his wife, Zia Raffaela, an exceptionally warm, and loving woman. My uncle Domenic was young, friendly, and confident.

We climbed on a very large sixties car, and left the train station. We may have gone immediately nearby to my aunt Maria's, and uncle Saro's house in one of the older parts of downtown Montreal, named Saint Antoine, near downtown Montreal. We were later met by bubbly Zio Filippo, Zia Lisa, and their two children, Mike and Josephine.

We lived there about a month, while my father underwent a barber's test, so as to start working in his profession. He learned a few basic French, and English expressions, and then found a benevolent older, English-speaking employer who gave him the opportunity to practice his trade.

While there, I had to get used to a new kind of panorama; not the beautiful green valleys, and the mesmerizing Mediterranean–a testimony to God's greatness–but tall, and proud skyscrapers, a testimony to human ingenuity–and pride.

That Summer, my cousins, and I visited the nearby skyscrapers often. We especially liked visiting them on the weekend, when very few people were around, and when we could safely slide down the long armrests of the escalators, without attracting adult attention. We also enjoyed going up and down Place Ville Marie's elevators, until, one day, we were firmly asked by a security guard to eave and never to return; which we did.

Downtown Montreal. For the first few weeks, we lived in an old house in St. Antoine. This area, where some Calabrians first lived, is now covered with high-rises. (S. Lacasse)

We left my Aunt Maria's house, after about one month and moved to a small, ground-floor apartment in Ville Emard, on the outskirts of the Montreal. Right across was a take-out restaurant with an ever-rotating giant basket, on a tall, thin, metal pillar. It had an unusual name: Kentucky Fried Chicken.

I became very close to my newly-found cousins. They all had very original personalities: Mike (the oldest), uncle Domenic's son, was the leader and we often followed him in getting ourselves into new adventures–and some trouble. Mike (the second oldest) my Uncle Filippo's son, was very bright, and had a way of reinforcing the oldest Mike's adventurous spirit. Little Rocco, the youngest of the group, was bright, and vivacious, but was compelled by his age to simply follow along. Josie, my younger, lovable cousin, inspired much teasing. Julia was from youth an unbelievable dynamo. Little Rocky was born, not long after our arrival. He was a gorgeous child, with energy and spunk that stayed with him to this day.

My first school was Holy Cross, a tall, dark, gray brick building. There, I was shielded by my cousins, and the Catholic atmosphere. Within months, I moved to a local, public, high school, again with my cousins; but we were in different grades, so I was left to fend for myself.

Like déjà vu, one late Fall day, one year and one half after our arrival, my father showed up at my school, and I was called down to the office. My father had already told the secretary that we were moving to Toronto. Montreal had shut its doors to my father's dream of opening his own barber shop. His English, and French were simply insufficient to pass the test required for a license that would have permitted him to own his own business.

But my father had done his homework. The province of Ontario was less demanding. In Toronto he could open his own business with a simple barber's license, which he already had. We left French Canada behind, and left most of our family behind, as well. In Toronto, I only had one uncle and a few cousins I didn't know. My coin, my faithful friend, was with me, and I protected it – *jealously*.

TORONTO AND BEYOND

Of course, we moved close to my uncle Rocco. There I

became close to my other cousins: Mike, Angela, and Palma. Ossington Avenue was on the edge of Little Italy

From there, I daily went to another Catholic middle school. I lived in an Italian area and, therefore, went to a predominantly Italian school.

The family grew again with the birth of my nephew, Nino and my niece, Lucy.

My years at Oakwood Collegiate were followed by studies at a liberal arts college in California, followed by more studies at Toronto's York University.

After graduation, I married my beautiful wife, Leonilda. Part-time studies followed to complete a Master's degree in Psychology. Six fulfilling years doing psychotherapy in a youth and family clinic ensued. My first children, Anthony, and Julie were born. For three years we lived in Rome, and then came back to Canada. Victor was born. Finally the decision to teach and counsel at the high-school level, and of teaching psychology, part-time, at the College level.

Those were at times trying, and at times joyful years. Throughout those years, my ancient coins remained my special treasure. Every time I opened the small metal box to look at, and touch them, I would mentally return back home to my carefree childhood years in my beloved Capistrano; and I did so whenever possible .

The Royal Cinema, College Street (Little Italy): One of four Toronto cinemas where Italian movies were shown regularly. (SimonP)

The Capistrano Committee of Toronto. The yearly Mothers' Day party organized by them for the Capistrano community, and friend.

4. UNCOVERING THE PAST

Many years after the above events, while counseling in a high school in Malton, near the Toronto airport, I decided the time had come to confirm if my coin was indeed a "Sextersius," and when, and by whom it had been minted. I sought through various web sites, and finally the amazing surprise: I found my coin on a web site on ancient coins.

I stared at the screen in disbelief. There was no doubt about it –*it was my coin*. Then the details: it was an ancient coin from the Greek-speaking, Roman colony of Hipponium, or Valentia (formerly Hipponion) on the west-central side of Calabria, the region I came from. In fact the Hipponium area was on a straight line only about 15 kilometers away from my town.

I looked closely for a date, but there was no date. There was no mention of the type of coin it was, nor was there any explanation of the identity of the female head I had looked at for decades. I was quite pleased to have found some details, but I had to wait many more years to finally find out the most important details.

A MIND-OPENING BOOK

In 1977, probably as a gift for completing university, my parents paid for my ticket to go back home. Almost exactly ten years had elapsed, and I was elated to go back and see my town, and family and friends again. It was one of the most blissful and unforgettable times of my life. I had changed; my friends had changed; even the town had changed somewhat.

I believe it was during that visit, that I found a book written by a local historian on the history of my town. The book was titled, *Capistrano, Ieri ed Oggi* (*Capistrano, Yesterday and Today*). The author, Dr. Giovanni Manfrida, was a top-notch academic. He had been a teacher, a Mayor in our town and finally the Superintendent of schools in our area of the Region of Calabria. The book was exceptionally well written–*and fascinating.*

Over the years, I read the book, or sections thereof, several times, and every time I had been fascinated by the events and people described in it. I protected the book with almost as much passion as my coin collection.

As a child, I had been told by my mother that the people from our town had moved inland centuries before from a fortress city on the mountain adjacent to the Mediterranean Sea one could see clearly from my town. The city was named Rocca Angitola (The Angitola Fortress). The book confirmed that fact–and added many more.

It also made evident that my people, and the people who had created the towns nearby had experienced many anguishing and tragic historical events. My coin, most probably, had been in the possession of various people through the centuries, as they faced the many nightmarish events described in the book.

As in all other areas of the world, regular epidemics had swept through Calabria, and had killed countless people. Malaria had been very common, as were other diseases that ravaged young and old. But, to my surprise, for centuries earthquakes had been the most terrifying curse to oppress my people.

Dr. Giovanni Manfrida: A highly respected academic and historian, author of Capistrano Ieri ed Oggi.

5. EARTHQUAKES: CALABRIA'S ONGOING APOCALYPSE

⊐⊏⊏⊏⊏≺

Ever since my people moved into Calabria centuries ago, earthquakes have regularly added to their sorrows, devastating their towns at relatively brief intervals. The most recent, damaging earthquake took place in 1947. Some houses in Capistrano were damaged, but there were no casualties. Other towns were damaged as well, but unlike previous strong earthquakes, it had reaped few lives, having been only eight on the Mercalli Scale (6.5 on the Richter Scale). But Calabria had not been that fortunate during previous earthquakes.

In 1908 the area between Messina, Sicily, and Reggio Calabria was hit by a devastating quake, and an ensuing tsunami which devastated the area, and killed between 60,000 and 120,000 people.[xiii] Even though quite distant from the epicenter, my village was severely affected, and several homes were destroyed. As in other Southern Calabrian towns, several large "baracche;" (shack-like structures) were hastily built to accommodate the surviving, homeless families. They lived in those primitive conditions for many years, until the government finally built decent, and comfortable dwellings for them, decades later.

"Le Baracche": One of several wooden shacks built for homeless families, after the 1908 earthquake. Many Calabrians in other damaged towns lived in similar shelters for many years.

Just three years before, on September 8, 1905, a strong earthquake struck Calabria, from Cosenza, in Northern Calabria, to Reggio, in the deepest south. The exact epicenter is not known, but it appears to have been somewhere between Vibo Valentia, and Nicastro, in Central Calabria. Over 600 people were killed, and about 3000 were wounded.[xiv] The city of Monteleone (today's Vibo Valentia) suffered significant damages.[xv]

Parghelia, a town located about 5 Kilometers southeast of Vibo Valentia, was totally devastated. The terrifying event was described by a local student to a visiting news reporter. It is very descriptive of what happened in various towns in Central Calabria.

It happened around 2:45 in the morning. Suddenly we

were awakened by a horrendous roar. It seemed as though all of hell had come upon our poor homes… Looking outside was futile as one could see nothing, given the dust that was rising from the ruins. The dust slowly settled and we were finally able to see each others' faces; We were all outside on the road, some with a shirt on, some with only pants on; some were wrapped in a bed sheet, and some, fully naked, were hiding in a corner trying to hide their nakedness. Meanwhile one could hear desperate cries, sobbing and people begging for help. In a corner a woman, almost naked, was yelling desperately, and she had undone her braids, and was covering her bare breasts with her hair. Another one…was digging through a mountain of ruins from which she said she could hear her daughter's voice that was later found alive. Another one… was holding the dead body of one of her children. A poor old man was hanging from a window with his legs stuck inside. He was begging to be freed from death and, in fact, he did die. And there were a hundred more pitiful cases.[xvi]

The town of Monterosso Calabro, just about 2-3 Kilometres from Capistrano, on a straight line, also suffered great damage. Nello Manduca, a local historian, shares with us in his book, *Arsura (Thirst)* that his town was "shattered" by a violent earthquake which destroyed the town and killed several inhabitants. The surviving habitants had to take cover in the country taking cover in shacks. [xvii]

No doubt, significant damages occurred also next door, in my village, and surrounding towns.

Parghelia; immediately after the 1905 earthquake.

Journalist, Luigi Barzini, wrote the following heart-rending description, September 1905, while visiting the afflicted area in Calabria:

> In this area people are dying of hunger and thirst...the help brought in with difficulty is not enough. The healthy need bread; the wounded need meat; water is missing, the dying need medical help...twenty thousand people have lost everything and do not even have containers to get water at the fountains. They are silent multitudes that cannot detach themselves from the ruins of their homes,

where their beloved died and that dazed wait without strength for the help that never comes.[xviii]

Sant'Onofrio, another well known town in my area, was visited, not long after the earthquake, by the Italian King and Ferraris, one of his ministers.

He was moved by the extent of the disaster, and the traumatized crowds that surrounded him. "It's horrible," he said later to his accompanying minister. Some women approached the King and said to him, "Your majesty, we lost everything; we no longer have a home, we have no possessions, we have no relatives. You only are left and God. Help us!"[xix] The King was moved.

During the month of November, 1894, a strong quake damaged Messina and Reggio Calabria, and killed about 100 people, wounding about one thousand others, and causing great damage.[xx]

Going back in time, on November 4, 1870, a "violent" earthquake hit my area of Central Calabria, and it was felt in all of Southern Italy and Western Sicily. It caused a large amount of damage, and it killed around 500 people.[xxi]

"THE SCOURGE": THE CATACLYSMIC EARTHQUAKES OF 1783

The most damaging earthquakes Calabria in recent centuries took place in 1783. On February 5, my village was severely damaged by a powerful quake. It was later *totally* destroyed on March 28 of the same year.[xxii] Fortunately, because of the constant tremors, the villagers had moved into the countryside, and only two people were killed. They were, though, left without homes, and had to later re-build from scratch.[xxiii]

More in-depth research about the 1783 earthquakes revealed a shocking fact: that year all of Calabria had been hit by a *series* of *devastating* earthquakes. In all, 949 major and minor quakes hit Calabria during three horrifying years an author appropriately called, "An Apocalypse."[xxiv] Others referred to it as "The Scourge" (God's Great Punishment).

Around 200 cities and towns were destroyed. The estimated number of deaths ranges from 32,000 to 50,000. The number of injured is unknown, though it must have been vast. The damage to property was incalculable. The quakes were so strong that some olive groves, and parts of villages slid kilometers down valleys. New valleys and lakes were created and the morphology of Calabria was transformed.[xxv]

Between 1783 and 1787, because of ongoing seismological changes, 215 new lakes of various sizes were created in the Region. This contributed to new epidemics which killed more people that those already killed by the earthquakes.[xxvi]

Several towns were never reconstructed, such as Isca, Castel Monardo, near my town, and Oppido. The people of Isca, on the east side of Calabria, built another town nearby, while the people of Castel Monardo built a new, exceptionally well-planned town, not far away from the first, which they named Filadelfia (The City of Brotherly Love), a name offered by their illustrious Bishop,

Giovanni Andrea Serrao.[xxvii] (You may read the fascinating history of this amazing city later on in this book).

Pietro Colletta, a writer of the time, left us a vivid description of the catastrophic events of 1783.

> On February 5, Wednesday, nearly an hour after noon, the ground shook…for one hundred seconds: …it killed thirty-two-thousand men of each sex and age, rich and noble, poor and plebeians…houses collapsed…. trees…were swallowed up, others were broken and overturned. [xxviii]

Colletta also recorded dramatic morphological changes in various areas of Southern Calabria. He summarizes the nightmare with the following chilling statement: "Nothing remained of the old forms; lands, cities, roads, signs vanished…Many works of nature and man, built over the centuries…were in a moment destroyed."[xxix]

Elia Serrao, a nobleman from Castel Monardo, in Central Calabria, who lived through that horrendous time, shares with us the disturbing details in his work, "Earthquakes in Calabria."

> Who can recount all the effects, and the phenomena and the new and strange things that afflicted us that we saw in that most miserable of times?

> They are without number, and filled with tears and beyond any human belief. Those quakes created by

superior powers, be it natural or unnatural…in every way scourged the miserable earth. They brought down even the most solid of palaces; they cracked marble slabs and rocks of great sizes ... Nothing resisted them, and the ground under our feet, swaying as the tempestuous sea, would not permit that humans would stay standing and fearfully pushed them back and forth. There was so much horror that each one supposed that the end of the world had come and that the earth, the water, and the rest of the heavens and of the ancient world would all mix together into chaos.

The earth in many places opened up and created horrendous chasms.

Some talk of mountains that disappeared….

Other mountains united and covered the valleys between them. The rivers that flowed over them, having no longer any exit point created new and large lakes. Furthermore, new springs appeared as old ones dried up. The night of the fifth of February, the sea on the Scilla Coast became higher and fuller and, having risen to a shocking height, buried a great number of humans who had ran to take refuge by the sea. Many workers with their oxen and other animals where found large distances away from where they had been working, while others were swallowed up by chasms that opened suddenly.

Many houses, many farms…traveled large distances and were found far away from their original location.

Oh how many valiant men, how many beautiful women, how many handsome young people were oppressed by a sudden and miserable ruin.

Oh how many superb buildings, how many temples, how many monasteries, which were the marvels of the world, were flattened to the ground.

How many memorable families, how many great inheritances, how many famous riches were left without inheritors![xxx]

In another work titled, "Earthquakes in our Province," Serrao describes the horrors that befell the people of my area of Central Calabria.

The look of our Province in that very terrible time was so miserable. One would see desolate and broken lands.

One could hear the moans of those who were left under the ruins. Some ran and in running found their death. Others tried to pull out of the ruins their languishing ones and the possessions dearest to them! The fathers and the mothers hugged their children as though they were about to lose them. Others offered peace and tried to reconcile with their enemies. Some confessed their sins in public...

...all was filled with death, confusion, pain, horror, ruin and desolation.[xxxi]

The ruins of various hamlets, and towns destroyed in that tragic period are still there to witness to the devastation of the earthquakes of 1783. Much of Calabria had to be re-built from scratch, and a special fund was created by the government of Southern Italy called, "La Cassa Sacra" (The Sacred Fund) for that very purpose.[xxxii]

Unfortunately, in spite of the devastating effect the 1783 earthquakes had on Calabria, only a very few Calabrians know of their occurrence, and impact. It's as if Calabrians chose to erase that period from their collective memory. Only now, with the advent of the Internet, it is on occasion mentioned, briefly, in the history section of some town's web sites. To my knowledge, no monument exists in Calabria to commemorate the time when most of Calabria's past was erased, and when its people had to start anew.

ISTORIA
DE' TREMUOTI

Avvenuti nella Provincia della Calabria ulteriore,
e nella Città di Meſſina

NELL'ANNO 1783.

E di quanto nella Calabria fu fatto per lo ſuo
riſorgimento fino al 1787.

Preceduta da una Teoria, ed Iſtoria Generale de' Tremuoti

DI

GIOVANNI VIVENZIO

CAVALIERE DELL' ORDINE REGALE, E MILITARE
COSTANTINIANO DI S. GIORGIO

Primo Medico delle LL. MM., Direttore de' Regali Militari Spedali delle Sicilie,
e delle pubbliche Cattedre di Fiſica Sperimentale, Medicina Pratica, Anatomia,
Oſtetricia, e Chirurgia, e Protomedico Generale del Regno.

*Membro dell' Accademia Imperiale delle Scienze di Pietroburgo, delle Società Reali
di Medicina di Parigi, e Patriotica di Milano, Socio, e Cenſore
dell' Accademia Regale degli Speculatori di Lecce, ec.*

VOLUME PRIMO.

NAPOLI MDCCLXXXVIII.
NELLA STAMPERIA REGALE.

*Historia De' Tremuoti...(The History of Earthquakes...) by G.
Vivenzio. Published in 1788. It details the damage caused by the
1783 earthquakes to most Calabrian towns and cities.*

DE' TREMUOTI. PARTE II. 171.

Stato di MAJORATO.

Majorato , Capiftrano , e Montefanto .

Quefto Stato fu intieramente diftrutto dal Tremuoto de' 28 *Marʒo* , i cui edificj foffrirono, principalmente in *Montefanto* gran danno , anche nelle prime fcoffe , cagionandovi molte fenditure nel fuolo , su cui poggiavano , per cui non più nell' antico fuolo , ma nel piano detto del *Monaftero* verrà tale Terra riedificata . Il territorio di quefto Stato produce . Vettovaglie di ogni genere , Olio , Lino , e Seta .

Stato di FILOGASO.

Filogafo , e Panaja .

Quefto Stato fu totalmente diftrutto ; e fra gli edificj rovinati fono da notarfi il Monaftero de' *Domenicani* nel primo , e de' *Cappuccini* nel fecondo . Tanto in *Filogafo* , che in *Panaja* fi vedevano nel territorio delle grandi fenditure , e qualche dilamazione . I prodotti del terreno confiftono in Frutta , e Vettovaglie di ogni genere ; ma la Popolazione non bafta per la coltura de' campi .

Y 2   *Stato*

Reproduction from Vivenzio's book, mentioned above. It testifies to the painful truth that the 1783 earthquakes "totally destroyed" my village, Capistrano, and the adjacent towns of Maierato, Montesanto, Filogaso and Panaja.

Remains of buildings in Castel Monardo. The city was totally destroyed by the 1783 earthquakes, and was never rebuilt.

MORE CATACLYSMS

Though the 1783 earthquakes may have been the most cataclysmic to hit all of Calabria, previous earthquakes had been very violent as well.

Moving back through the historical layers, one finds more destruction and horror. The year 1659 was another destructive year for Calabria, and for my area in particular. V. D'Amato informs us that 1659 was a "bitter" year for Calabria. The fifth of November the ground trembled with "great violence." He specifically mentions Castel Monardo, Polia, Monterosso and Capistrano as having being particularly affected. [xxxiii]

Giovanni Manfrida, in his book, *Capistrano Ieri ed Oggi*, confirms the painful truth that Capistrano was severely affected by that earthquake. More specifically, 16 people were killed; forty houses were destroyed, including the largest church.[xxxiv]

The number of Calabrians killed by that earthquake was about 2000. The number of people who were injured is unknown.[xxxv]

Just twenty one years before, in March of 1638, Central and Southern Calabria had been hit by three other damaging earthquakes. Calabrian Count, Francesco Ippolito, in his letter to the English Nobleman, Sir William Hamilton, referring to the two, above-mentioned destructive periods, wrote the following: "Calabria has been at all times exposed to the terrible convulsions of which we are at present the victims. The earthquakes in 1638 and 1659, by which two provinces of Calabria were utterly destroyed, are fresh in every one's memory..."[xxxvi]

How destructive were they? The available sources estimate that 180 cities and towns were destroyed[xxxvii] A great many Calabrians were killed.

> "The nation was again afflicted with a most terrible A.D. 1638 earthquake which, on the 27th of March, destroyed a great many cities in Calabria. Cosenza, Castiglione, Nicastro, and many other cities, and a great number of villages were almost entirely reduced to ruins, and above ten thousand people were killed."[xxxviii]

This tragic number is confirmed by Pier Paolo Poggio in his *Storia Sociale della Calabria* (*A Social History of Calabria*). He informs us that in 1638 the earthquake partially destroyed many habitations in Cosenza, Briatico, Castelfranco, Castiglione, Pietramola, Nocera and Nicastro. The victims were about 10,000."[xxxix] Others, instead, estimate that the casualties were between 10,000 and 30,000.[xl]

The earthquakes extended south into my area, and all the way dow n into the southernmost province of Reggio Calabria.

Athanasius Kircher, an esteemed Jesuit writer and scholar of the time who was visiting Sicily and Calabria when the earthquakes struck, describes what he experienced in very descriptive and chilling language.

> Having hired a boat, in company with four more (two friars of the order of St. Francis, and two seculars) we

launched from the harbor of Messina, in Sicily; and arrived, the same day, at the promontory of Pelourus. Our destination was for the city of Euphaemia, in Calabria, where we had some business to transact, and where we designed to tarry for some time.

(Author's Note: Euphaemia was located in the general area of Lamezia Terme of today, located in Central Calabria.

The sea itself seemed to wear a very unusual appearance: they who have seen a lake in a violent shower of rain, covered all over with bubbles, will conceive some idea of its agitations. My surprise was still increased, by the calmness and serenity of the weather; not a breeze, not a cloud, which might be supposed to put all nature thus into motion. I therefore warned my companions, that an earthquake was approaching; and, after some time, making for the shore with all possible diligence, we landed at Tropea, happy and thankful for having escaped that threatening dangers of the sea.

But our triumphs at land were of short durations; for we had scarcely arrived at the Jesuits' College, in that city, when our ears were stunned with a horrid sound, resembling that of an infinite number of chariots, driven fiercely forward; the wheels rattling, and thongs cracking. Soon after this, a most dreadful earthquake ensued; the whole tract upon which we stood seemed to vibrate, as if we were in the scale of a balance that continued wavering. This motion, however, soon grew more violent; and being no longer able to keep my legs, I was thrown prostrate upon the ground. In the mean time, the universal ruin round me doubled my amazement.

The crash of falling houses, the tottering of towers, and the groans of the dying, all contributed to raise my terror and despair. On every side of me, I saw nothing but a scene of ruin...it was all silence, and a gloomy dread of impending terrors.

Leaving this seat of desolation, we prosecuted our voyage along the coast; and the next day came to Rochetta, where we landed, although the earth still continued in violent agitations. But we had scarcely arrived at our inn, when we were once more obliged to return to the boat; and, in about half an hour, we saw the greater part of the town, and the inn which we had put up, dashed to the ground, and burying the inhabitants beneath the ruins.

(Author's Note: Kircher appears to refer to the town of Briatico, a coastal town near Pizzo Calabro, about 10 Km. from the Angitola River.

In this manner, proceeding onward in our little vessel, finding no safety at land, and yet, from the smallness of our boat, having but a very dangerous continuance at sea, we were bound. Here, wherever I turned my eyes, nothing but scenes of ruin and horror appeared; towns and castles leveled to the ground;

Stromboli, though at sixty miles distance, belching forth flames in an unusual manner, and with a noise which I could distinctly hear.

But my attention was quickly turned from more remote, to contiguous danger. The rumbling sound of an approaching earthquake, which we by this time were grown acquainted with, alarmed us for the consequences; it every moment seemed to grow louder, and to approach nearer. The place on which we stood now began to shake most dreadfully: so that being unable to stand, my companions and I caught hold of whatever shrub grew next to us, and supported ourselves in that manner.

After some time, this violent paroxysm ceasing, we again stood up, in order to prosecute our voyage to Euphaemia, which lay within sight. In the mean time, while we were preparing for this purpose, I turned my eyes toward the city, but could see only a frightful dark cloud, that seemed to rest upon the place. This the more surprised us, as the weather was so very serene.

We waited, therefore, till the cloud had passed away: then turning to look for the city it was totally sunk. Wonderful to tell! Nothing but a dismal and putrid lake was seen where it stood. We looked about to find someone that could tell us of its sad catastrophe, but could see no person. All was become a melancholy solitude; a scene of hideous desolation.

Thus proceeding pensively along, in quest of some human being that could give us a little information, we at length saw a boy sitting by the shore, and appearing stupefied with terror. Of him, therefore, we inquired concerning the fate of the city; but he could not be prevailed on to give us an answer.

We entreated him, with every expression of tenderness and pity, to tell us; but his senses were quite wrapped up in the contemplation of the danger he had escaped. We offered him some victuals, but he seemed to loath the sight. We still persisted in our offices of kindness; but he only pointed to the place of the city, like one out of his senses; and then running up into the woods, was never heard of after. Such was the fate of the city of Euphaemia.

As we continued our melancholy course along the shore, the whole coast, for the space of two hundred miles, presented nothing but the remains of cities; and men scattered without a habitation, over the fields. Proceeding thus along, we at length ended our distressful voyage by arriving at Naples, after having escaped a thousand dangers both at sea and land.[xli]

Kircher describes Aeuphemia as having sunk, and as having been replaced by a lake. That was an assumption based on what he saw. In reality, we now know that the town had been destroyed by an unforgiving tsunami that buried the town, and an unknown number of its inhabitants with its high waves.

The people who survived moved more inland, and built a city on a nearby hill named Sant'Eufemia. Today, the city has joined together with the nearby Sembiase, and Nicastro to create the new, prosperous, airport city of Lamezia Terme.

The layers before the 1600's are vague, and the details more sparse. Historian Serrao, from the town of Castel Monardo, assures us that his town was destroyed three times before the 1500's, and that great damage was also caused in that town in 1184.[xlii] We can safely assume that the same fate befell nearby towns, and probably most or all of Calabria as well.

No doubt many more earthquakes leveled the villages in the area during the first millennium A.D., but I have not been able to find any reliable records of those tragic events.

A LINGERING ANXIETY

These unstoppable, destructive events have done much to shape the mental set of Calabrians. There is a belief in many of my people that nothing is really solid; nothing is there to last. A lingering anxiety resides in the mind of many of them that steals from them the mental peace they so much need and crave.

This view is also held by Dr. Vito Teti, a professor at the University of Calabria, and an expert in Calabrian Anthropology. According to Dr. Teti, to Calabrians life and material possessions are framed by "temporariness," and by a firmly-held belief that "nothing lasts." [xliii]

Unfortunately, this belief is grounded on centuries of evidence which point to an inevitable reality: the future has in store more painful times for my people. Earthquakes are not just a part of their past–*they are an inevitable part of their future*–and they must accept this painful challenge with total determination, so as to make sure that future damage will be as limited as possible. This can be accomplished by imposing stringent building codes, and by educating young and old on how to survive, if and when another series of powerful quakes will hit our beloved land.

CONCERN FOR MY PEOPLE

The knowledge of the above, chilling facts, in time gave rise to much anxiety, and concern for my people. The facts spoke clearly, and they were quite foreboding. Since 1638, Calabria has been hit by very powerful quakes, on average about every 65 years. Each time this occurred, the number of people killed was very high, and the damage to buildings had been vast and incalculable.

Since the last strong (but not very destructive) earthquake hit Calabria in 1947, if the trends of the past will repeat, one must deduce that a violent earthquake which will affect most, or all of Calabria, might be near.

To determine how near, I calculated how often, on average, Calabria was hit by destructive earthquakes (8 and above on the Mercalli Scale, and 6.5 and above on the Richter Scale). I then calculated the average for the three general areas of Calabria: North, Centre and South. Afterwards, I proceeded to add the Region-wide average with the local ones, and came up with an average for each of the three main geographic areas.

The diagrams on the next page make it clear that there is much to be concerned about.

DESTRUCTIVE EARTHQUAKES THAT AFFECTED ALL OF CALABRIA, AND CENTRAL CALABRIA SINCE 1638.

AVERAGE: EVERY 61.8 YEARS

....

DESTRUCTIVE EARTHQUAKES THAT AFFECTED ALL OF CALABRIA, AND NORTHERN CALABRIA SINCE 1638.

AVERAGE: EVERY 65.6 YEARS

....

DESTRUCTIVE EARTHQUAKES THAT AFFECTED ALL OF CALABRIA, AND SOUTHERN CALABRIA SINCE 1638.

AVERAGE: EVERY 67.5 YEARS

Another fact which became of concern to me was the time of year when most of the powerful quakes occurred. Most took place during the cold, and wet months, as made evident by the diagram on the next page.

MONTH	FREQUENCY	LOCATION
January	0	
February	3	(1783, 1783 All) / (1743, Southern)
March	4	(1638, 1783, All) / (1783, Central) / (1832, Croton area)
April	1	(1836, North)
May	1	(1947, Central)
June	2	(1913, North) / (1638, Croton area)
July	0	
August	0	
September	1	(1905, All)
October	4	(1791, Central) / (1835,Cosenza) / (1870, Cosenza) / (1907, South)
November	2	(1659, Central) / (1894, South)
December	2	(1887, North) / (1908, South)

A TIME FOR ACTION

The above realizations created in me much concern. For some time, I felt powerless and my sleep was affected by images of destruction. I had studied this dark side of my people's history in greater depth than most Calabrians, and I felt that I was in possession of a dark secret which my people needed to be aware of–*and were not.* I decided to inform my immediate friends back home, by using the very active Guestbook on our town's web site. I shared most of the relevant evidence with them, hoping for concern, followed by constructive actions; instead, the Guestbook went suddenly almost silent. I believe the day after one realistic guest wrote that given the evidence there was much to worry about. Another one suggested that there was no need for much concern since the situation would have been handled competently by the state department that dealt with such disasters. One or two tried to turn the whole thing into something humorous.

Their response was clearly understandable. The picture I painted for them was worrisome. Being away from the area, I could look at the whole scenario with some detachment. The ones who live in Calabria have to confront a reality that is simply too scary to confront. Thus, many retreated into silence, while a few others tried to turn it into humor.

Ironically, not long after I informed the Guestbook guests of the impending quakes, a series of tremors hit Central Calabria, and my area. That immediately brought sobriety into the dialogue. A friend from our town wrote in to inform us. All were shaken, but the fear led to almost total silence on the Guestbook for days.

In the meantime, I decided that I had to do more than just inform the people of my town. I went on to create a web site in Italian which would inform Calabrians of all the facts I had uncovered, with a detailed section on what to do in case of earthquakes. The web site is titled, *Terremoti in Calabria (Earthquakes in Calabria)*.

I had one fear, though: would the facts lead them to immediately react with the well known psychological defense mechanism of "Denial"? Whatever their reaction, I felt I had to do my part–*my conscience demanded it.*

In time, the web site gained momentum. Close to ten thousands have visited the site, as of May 2013.

Best of all, I have been contacted by a Facebook group of concerned local citizens who are also trying to reach our people, and warn them of the impending danger. We have now joined forces and, with time and determination, we hope to reach large numbers of our people, and especially regional government leaders who hopefully will join us in our quest.

The Stromboli Volcano: Located very near the coasts of Sicily and Calabria. Just north of it, located about 400 meters below sea level, is the Marsili Volcano, potentially very dangerous to all of Southern Italy, given its capacity to create destructive tsunamis.
(Janot)

6. NAPOLEON: THE SCOURGE FROM THE NORTH

This detail in my village, and Calabria's history was discovered late in my search. It had been mentioned, very briefly, in Manfrida's work, but in a limited historical context. In time, and with the help of various other sources, I was able to put the pieces together and make sense of this other major trauma that befell several Calabrian towns.

In 1806, Napoleon's forces conquered Southern Italy with little effort. Over time, thousands of Calabrians, supplied with arms by the British, rebelled against the oppressive foreign rulers, and attacked Napoleon's soldiers whenever they could. The casualties were high, on both sides. The Calabrian rebels fought ferociously. Napoleon's commanders responded with vengeance and brutality.

Gregory Desmond informs us that the most intense revolts took place in both Abbruzzi and Calabria, from 1806 to 1811. The French fought to suppress the rebels for five years, at the cost of 20,000 casualties. General Reynier, was pursued by 8,000 Calabresi, and he responded by sacking, and burning every village in the way to keep them from providing assistance to the rebels.[xliv]

Reynier was later replaced by General Messéna whose task was that of *crushing* the revolt. Reynier forced local municipalities to finance his army, took over the property of the rebel leaders, closed monasteries which he believed were providing assistance to the rebels, sacked the town of Lauria after having held out against his army, and reoccupied Cosenza. [xlv]

Napoleon's advice to his brother, Joseph, who ruled Italy under him, was to be strong, harsh and unforgiving. The following is a portion of his letter to his brother detailing how Southern Italians were to be treated.

> There must be no forgiveness. Have at least 600 rebels shot…Burn down the houses of thirty of the principal inhabitants in the villages, and share out their property to the army. Disarm the people and have five or six large villages given over to pillage. Give away the communal property from the rebel villages and give 11 to the army. [xlvi]

An unknown number of rebels who opposed Napoleon's army, led by their leader, Papasidero, took refuge in my village, and there the French general, Lucotte, attacked and defeated them. One hundred and fifty rebels were killed. Capistrano was later sacked by the troops. [xlvii] The fight took place from house to house and finally, as punishment, the town was burned, and razed to the ground. The rebels who survived disappeared in the nearby mountains. [xlviii]

Capistrano was a small village with a population of about one thousand people, in those days. Seeing hundreds of anxious rebels approach the village may have been perplexing for many. Seeing, afterwards, a large numbers of determined French soldiers enter the village must have been terrifying.

Some local young men may have joined the rebels to fight the foreigners. A large number of cautious villagers may have hid far away. Some may have watched the battle from the safety of the nearby mountain. The battle must have been fierce, and the gun battle must have been deafening, as hundreds of gun shots echoed through the surrounding valleys. After a brutal and bloody struggle, the gun shots finally came to a end.

Upon reflecting upon the events of that time, it dawned on me that, after the battle, the streets I know so well, that I played in as a child, were strewn with dead, and injured bodies. If 150 rebels were killed, how many of Napoleon's soldiers met the same fate? How many rebels were captured, and then massacred, so as to teach other rebels a lesson, as Napoleon demanded? Lastly, how many villagers were caught in the cross fire and killed?

That fateful day, blood was flowing down the steep St. Antonio road, in the piazza, in Via Zotta, in the Via Tripona and especially down the Corso. Some of the houses in which my people still live in today may have been strewn with lifeless bodies. The blood-curdling cries of severely wounded rebels, and many of Napoleon's soldiers, filled the air. Death embraced Capistrano that day, and held many to its cold, dark chest and carried them away.

On April 22nd, 1806 Napoleon wrote a letter to his brother to congratulate him for having burned down a village. It probably was not my village but, perhaps, the first of several Southern Italian villages that were yet to be destroyed. The following was Napoleon's attitude toward such senseless destruction, which he enjoined on his brother:

> My Brother,—I have received your letter of April 5th. I see with pleasure that an insurgent village has been burnt down. Severe examples are necessary. I suppose the village has been given over to the soldiers for plunder. That is the way to treat all revolted villages. It is not only the right of war but a duty enjoined by Policy. (April 22nd, 1806).[xlix]

My village was to be one of the villages Napoleon condemned to destruction from another land. The senseless act was willed by a megalomaniac who cared little about human life, and human suffering, and who sought only glory for himself, and his family. My people were forced to rebuild the town, once again, just as they had done twenty-three years before, as a result of the 1783 earthquakes. And this they did with much patience and resilience.

Capistrano's campanile (bell tower). An ideal location from where rebels could have taken aim at Napoleon's soldiers.

Il Corso: An older, central part of town where much of the fighting probably took place.(M. Caputo)

7. THE VILLAGE BEGINS

According to Dr. Manfrida, the author of the Capistrano book, the village started about 1200 years ago when a small number of Basilian, Greek-speaking monks had left areas of the Byzantine Empire, and Sicily in particular, so as not to be under Muslim rule. They chose a location far away from the coast where they could work the land, and live their life of reflection, and prayer in relative safety.

They were part of a massive exodus of Basilian monks that moved to various parts of Calabria from different parts of the Byzantine Empire, as a result of Muslim conquests. In Calabria they created a large number of monasteries of various sizes.

But the monasteries led to another development: the creation of small communities of farmers that gathered around them and slowly grew, over the centuries, to become villages and towns.

As many other Calabrian villages, my village began as a small group of families gathered around the small abbey located on the north side of town in the area known today as, "La Batia," a derivative name of the Italian word "Badia," which means "Abbey."[1] It is also conceivable that a small hamlet may have already existed in the area, and that the monks settled near it. For certain, the arrival of the Basilian brothers led to further growth.

According to Manfrida, the group of monks must have been

small; perhaps two or three. Nevertheless, they would have provided comfort and solace for an anxious people that had moved away from the dangerous coast where Saracen attacks were common. In that safe location, they would have worked the promising land, while receiving spiritual nourishment from the monks.

Finally, my people would have experienced some peace. Many friends and families, though, chose to stay behind in the fortress on the Rocca Mountain, by the Angitola River, near the coast. Contact must have been relatively easy, and ongoing, due to the relative proximity of the two locations.

My coin may have been brought over by one of those struggling people, or, perhaps, it may have been the possession of someone in the Rocca Fortress, who was waiting to move inland later, when the need would have arisen.

"La Batia" Fountain. The village of Capistrano began in
this area, around the year 850 A.D. (M. Caputo)

Lower Capistrano, as seen today from the Batia area. This view
was drawn by Renoir, while in my village.(M. Caputo)

8. ROCCA ANGITOLA: THE UNRELENTING FORTRESS

Looking down toward the distant Mediterranean, from atop the various hills that rise on either side of the Angitola Valley, the onlooker's eyes are met, in the distance, with a mountain that blocks the view to most of the blue Mediterranean. This is the Angitola Mountain, a sacred place for thousands of people who live in the various towns that rest atop these hills.

Over the centuries, a great many parents that have lived in these small towns have accepted the sacred duty of passing on to their children the precious truth that all of us originate from that distant location.

My mother embraced that duty as well, many years ago and, when she thought that I was old enough to understand the concept of origins, she, like her mother or father had done before her, passed on to me the precious knowledge that our people, long time ago, had come from the Rocca Angitola (The Angitola Fortress).

It was not difficult for her to reinforce history with geography. From my house one only had to look out of our kitchen balcony and in the distance was the Angitola Mountain, and adjacent to it, the stunning Mediterranean.

She must have repeated the historical lesson more than once, as it was chiseled in my mind and has indelibly stayed with me since those distant days. In fact, for decades, if anyone would have asked me what was my greatest longing, the answer would have been, "To climb the Rocca Mountain, and visit the city where my ancestors came from."

Because there were no pictures or videos of the Rocca available to me in those days, I felt the need to create a mental image of what the ruins may have looked like. Strangely, my mental images were not of majestic ruins, but of a few dilapidated walls and scattered rocks in the green grass.

The fact that my mental image of the city was not that impressive did not really matter to me. The Rocca was the mother of all the towns in our area, and I needed to imagine something of my ancient mother, like an orphan needs to imagine his own mother, though the image may only be a creation.

With the advent of the Internet, and Google Earth, in particular, I tried to search for the city, looking from the sky for signs of ruins, but in vain. Finally my friend and relative from back home, Pino La Serra, who had visited the fortress, circled the area where it was located on a picture shot from above with Google Earth, and sent it to me.

His help made it clear that the reasons I was not able to find it were twofold: first of all, I had been looking in the wrong location and, secondly, the remains of the ancient city are barely visible.

In 2008, I casually searched the name, "Rocca Angitola," on the Internet and, to my joyful surprise, a site appeared which documented the pilgrimage of several people from nearby towns to the Rocca. The site also showed beautiful pictures of the ruins of the city. Finally, my eyes looked for the very first time at what for decades had been only a fantasy.

To my amazement, the place was much bigger than I thought, and the remains were clearly more impressive than the scattered rocks, and the few barely visible walls I had imagined.

In 2010, I had the opportunity to visit my town and, while there, I decided to fulfill my decades-old dream, and go visit the fortress in person, so as to take my own pictures and videos of the area. According to what I could see with Google Earth, accessing the Rocca looked easier than I had thought. But I was wrong!

My companion and guide was going to be my cousin, Angelo, who knew the area well. Unfortunately, due to a misunderstanding, my cousin did not make it to our appointment, and I ended up tackling the adventure on my own.

I left my town around 6:00 AM and, after a relatively short drive, I ended at the top of the Rocca Mountain. I parked and then walked down a dirt road toward my destination. After battling intense heat, and nasty flies for probably another 30-40 minutes, I reached the base of the Rocca cliff where the fortress was located.

For the first time, I stared with wonderment at the very steep incline, and looked up to a proud wall that had been built centuries ago to protect my people. After the effect of the magical and joyful moment waned, I suddenly realized that the task of entering the ancient city would have been much more arduous than I thought.

The very steep incline was covered with impenetrably-thick vegetation, and *a lot* of thorny vines.

I tried to climb the incline, just to give it a try, but within a few meters the attempt became exceptionally difficult, and I wisely decided not to go on.

I walked down the dirt road a few more minutes. I saw the ruins of an ancient, abandoned house, at the base of the incline. I looked up at the other walls I could barely see through the trees. I tried to climb again from another location, but in vain. I had to quickly get back down; the vegetation was simply impenetrable. I had forgotten why the Fortress had been built in that location. It was built in that location to protect the inhabitants from the invading, brutal Saracens, and, thus, it had to be hard to approach– and it surely was.

By around 9 AM, I gave it the last shot. By then it had become stifling hot; I was sweating profusely, and I was running out of water. I finally found what seemed to be a path leading to the fortress, and walked up a gentler incline for some time, but it, too, led to the usual thick vegetation and sharp thorny vines.

I finally decided to walk back to the dirt road but, for some still mysterious reason, I lost my way, and ended up in an area *abounding* with thorny vines. My return back to the dirt road was blocked by what seemed to be an impenetrable wall of trees, bushes and thorns.

It took me what seemed to be an eternity to finally work my way down to the dirt road I had come from, and my bare legs and arms were cut severely by the sharp thorns that seemed ready to fiercely protect the area from any intruders.

By 9:30, the adventure had already ended. The child who had longingly waited for decades to see his ancient mother was prevented from achieving his dream. It felt as if my mother was being kept prisoner behind the menacing walls, and I was being forcefully told to go away by an unknown force.

Disappointed, I took some pictures of the walls, and some videos of the very picturesque, surrounding area. I felt somewhat defeated, but I promised myself I would return next time, better prepared, and guided by someone who knew the area better than I did.

La Rocca Angitola is, indeed, the mother of thousands of inhabitants of several towns in the area. The people of Francavilla, Polia, Monterosso, Capistrano, San Nicola, Vallelonga, Filogaso and Maierato, etc. have their roots in that walled city, on that mountain which sheltered and protected our ancestors for hundreds of years.

It was a city that through its agonizing history saw little peace and much anguish. It's the city that we, its children need to learn more about. We also have to accept the sacred duty to pass on that knowledge to our children, as our parents have done through the centuries.

The following are some of major happenings that befell my ancestors who lived in that city over many centuries.

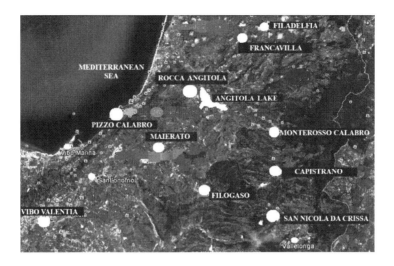

The Angitola Valley, its towns and nearby centers. (Google Earth)

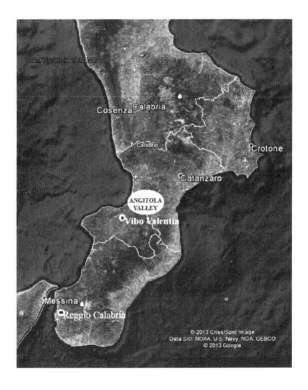

Rocca Angitola, and the Angitola Valley: Located in Central Calabria, in the Province of Vibo Valentia. (Google Earth).

AN INGLORIOUS END

Very few courageous and adventurous souls dare to tackle the challenge of climbing the steep incline which leads to the Rocca Fortress. The very few that do, after walking through the almost impenetrable vegetation, and the unforgiving thorny vines, will finally be rewarded with a first-hand look at what today is an ancient ghost town. Most of the buildings are nothing but ruins. Some churches, and the castle, have a few walls standing. What used to be bustling city streets today are a sea of thick bushes and ever-present thorns.

The fortress city did not simply deteriorate because of age. The roofs and walls did not simply cave in because of lack of care. The Rocca was totally destroyed by the cataclysmic earthquakes of 1783 which, as discussed above, destroyed upwards of 200 Calabrian cities and towns. But, unlike the other locations, the Rocca had already been officially declared abandoned, and uninhabited on February 2, 1772 by Giorgio Pirrone, a Notary Public from the nearby city of Pizzo Calabro, with the witness of several people who had accompanied him to the location. The document, which was written and testified to by the group, states that they had found only four small houses in livable condition and that these few remaining dwellings had been abandoned, and had been emptied of any possessions.

The document also records that the last inhabitants had left after the night of January 21, 1771, when some criminals had gone into the area and had killed a man by the name of Giuseppe Bova and wounded another man by the name of Martino Curigliano. The terrified leaders of the four remaining families decided that it was time to abandon the Rocca, and move to "...locations with a lot of inhabitants, and to run from that desert, where they continually see themselves harmed and assailed by such criminals and assassins."[li]

Ten years before, in 1762, fifteen people plus the priest were still living in the city.[lii] A document drafted by the Notary Public, Francesco Salomone, states that six inhabitants had spoken highly of their priest, Pasquale Malerba, who for six years had looked after the spiritual needs of the people of the area. The priest would live in the Rocca only from November to June. In the Summer months, he resided in the nearby Scrisi Plain from where he returned on Sundays and holy days to celebrate Mass. In March of that year, six criminals approached the people of the area and asked if the priest was a wealthy man. The six inhabitants, having understood their devious intents, warned the priest, and advised him to leave the area and move to the city of Pizzo Calabro, nearby, where he would have been safer.[liii]

Giuseppe Greco, the foremost historian of the Rocca, informs us that the three bells from the Santa Maria della Cattolica Church were transported to nearby Maierato, where they were placed in the bell tower of the main church.[liv] The crucifix, called commonly, "The Father of the Rocca," was brought to the church of San Giorgio in nearby Pizzo Calabro where it is worshiped to this very day.[lv]

But why was such a place abandoned, after so many years of

tortuous and heroic history? The main reason appears to have been malaria.

In the late 1600, a priest by the name of Martire wrote about the Rocca's already deplorable condition and the cause of the same.

> It had been a good land, all walled with towers…now, as I saw it in the year 1691, on the occasion of the visit, it was all in ruin, with few homes still standing and with very few people, there were only 50 souls and the thorns from the grasses almost fully covered it, being uninhabited because of malaria, caused by that river, even though abounding in trout and eels.[lvi]

Even before, in the late 1500's, the ancient Calabrian writer, Marafioti, had called the air of the area, "most unhealthy."[lvii] No doubt he was referring to the malaria causes by the mosquitoes which abounded in the area.

Giuseppe Greco, is also of the view that over the centuries the Angitola River nearby was the cause of the malaria.

> (The Angitola River) …flowing rapidly down the mountains carried wood, sand and mud, which by creating an obstacle for the flowing water, gave way, with the passing of time, to a swamp which, with the appearance of the Summer's heat, infected the air all around, causing deterioration in agriculture and tormenting fevers in the

population.^{lviii}

The great earthquakes of 1638 and 1659 had also done their part to bring the Rocca to its eclipse. According to a writer of the time, Lutio D'orsi, who visited the area after the 1638 earthquake, 33 houses had been destroyed, as was the upper part of the castle, but there were no deaths.^{lix}

Less destructive was the earthquake of 1659 when only eight houses were damaged, as was the Church of Santa Maria della Cattolica.^{lx}

All of the above events marked the inglorious end of a city which had survived centuries of invasions and natural disasters, and which had been one of the most strategically important locations in Calabria.

Unlike the previous two earthquakes, the earthquakes of 1783 were unforgiving, and totally wiped out the city and, in so doing, they erased a long era which had been a part of my history, and of the history of so many others living in the surrounding towns, and thousands more living in foreign lands.

THE PROSPEROUS YEARS

The declining years, going from the early 1600 to the late 1700, were preceded by relatively abundant and peaceful years. We are fortunate to have descriptions of the area from some of the best known Calabrian historians of the past, who paint a mental picture of a land rich in both agriculture and commerce.

The first Calabrian writer to describe the area was Gabriele

Barrio, who wrote the first historical work on Calabria titled, *De Antiquitate et Situ Calabriae,* written in classical Latin. In this work Barrio describes a productive and prosperous location.

> Then there is the Angitola Fortress in an elevated area, and the river by the same name, navigable, filled with fish and rich with trout and eels. ...Every year there is a famous Fair...In this location they grow sesame, and cotton, they extract marble, and in the internal areas one can also find sandstone; the salicaceae trees grow there... In this territory abound birds and game.[lxi]

Marafioti, another Calabrian writer of the 1500's gives us a similar description of the area.

> All the territory of the Rocca abounds in perfect wheat, sandstone, and there are marble cliffs...In the area near the river they grow sesame plants...In the country one can find various birds, and in particular partridges, pheasants and other birds of value.[lxii]

According to other documents of the time, the area produced an abundance of wheat, rye, fave beans, chickpeas, beans, flax, oil and wine.[lxiii] It was, in short, an area where the people could satisfy their basic needs, and leave in relative prosperity.

Massive walls which anciently protected the Rocca Fortress from invading forces. *(Giuseppe Maio)*

THE TYRANNICAL YEARS

Southern Italy was divided between the Spanish and the French, on November 2, 1500. Unfortunately, this deal was followed by a war between the two powers which was won by the Spanish in 1503, at the battle of Seminara, and later at Melfi, Garigliano and Cerignola.

One of the French military leaders found safety in the Rocca Angitola, after his defeat at Seminara in 1503.[lxiv] While there, he was surrounded by the Spanish. After a siege of an unknown length, the Spanish invited him to surrender and, once convinced that he, and his family would have received safe conduct, he finally came out.[lxv] We do not know if any, or much blood was spilled during the siege which preceded the surrender.

The nobles who owned the Rocca in those days were the Princes Alfonso and Honorato di Sanseverino, who participated in the war on the side of the French. They were captured and imprisoned until September 14, 1506, when they were finally released, but were spoiled of their possessions.

The member of the Spanish nobility who was rewarded with the Rocca was Diego de Mendoza, a member of a rich, noble Spanish family, for having fought bravely on the Spanish side at Barletta.

During this period, Southern Italy was governed by a Viceroy. Unfortunately, during this time Southern Italians were forced by the nobles to do unpaid work, and were treated like servants or slaves.[lxvi]

Taxation became oppressive, and abuse abounded. As Greco reminds us, the time of the Spanish rule, "...represents the saddest period of our history. From documents of the time we can garner acts of ferocity, oppression, and violence."[lxvii]

During this time, brigands also oppressed the Calabrian people. They controlled roads, and exacted a tribute for their use. This was also the case in the area of the Rocca where, according to tradition, a man by the name of San Bartolo was skinned alive, simply because he could not pay the required amount.[lxviii]

The population of the Rocca reached a sizeable number in those days. By 1561, 275 families lived in the Rocca, from only

141 in 1532. [lxix] Since families were composed of several members in those days, we can surmise that in 1561 the actual population of the city may have been between one to two thousands. Their life, though, was not easy, given the oppressive Spanish rule.

Probably the ancient remains of a church. (*Giuseppe Maio*)

THE OPPRESSIVE YEARS

Though the 1500's had been years of tyranny, the previous two centuries were not any better. A few nobles controlled all of Calabria, and they ruled their possessions as kings would have. They had judicial control, and could impose any tax they wanted. If the taxed could not afford to pay, they were imprisoned, or their possessions were taken away. [lxx]

In 1442, when Alfonso V, "The Magnanimous," became king

over Naples, the Aragonian rule over Southern Italy began. He replaced the taxes imposed by the previous ruler with a new tax named, "Focatico," which demanded ten Carlini from each family in the Kingdom. A salt tax was also added which brought the total amount to 15 Carlini. The taxes had to be paid in three amounts, at Christmas, Easter, and in September.[lxxi]

The feudal lords continued to oppress Calabria, and the Rocca people. In 1492, after the Camponeschi family rule ended, and the Sanseverino family took over the area, the inhabitants of the Rocca bemoaned the oppression of their previous lord who had forced them to pay 60 tomoli of wheat per year, and who had compelled them to use his mills with payment. Because the mills had become King's, they appealed to him to end the oppression.[lxxii]

In 1495 the area ended in the hands of the Count of Belcastro and the Roccans were forced to swear allegiance to him.[lxxiii]

It is during the early 1400's that the name Rocca Angitola replaced the old name, "Rocca Niceforo." In 1423, we are informed by documents of the time, that the possessions of Giovanni Caracciolo included an area called, Rocca Niceforo.[lxxiv] Not long after, the kingly order of October 7, 1425 to the Count of Buccino referred to the same location as, "Roccangitola"[lxxv]

In 1429, Queen Giovanna II gave as possession to Antonio de Camponeschis the area called, "Rocca Angitola."[lxxvi]

Thus, amidst all the oppression, the new name for the fortress emerged and became entrenched into history to our days.

THE LAURIA'S CENTURY

Little has come to us from the 1300's, except for the fact that the Lauria family became the undisputed rulers of the Rocca. Documents from the start of the century, (soon after 1302), reveal that the city belonged to the Grand Admiral, Ruggero di Lauria, a military leader who had been involved in many battles of the time.[lxxvii]

In 1310 the city became property of Ruggero's son, Carlo, and in 1313 it became the property of Berengario, Carlo's brother. Afterwards, the new lord of the area was the Count Arrigo Sanseverino Di Marsico, who married Maria di Lauria, the last inheritor of the Admiral Ruggero, mentioned above. The city was part of Maria's dowry.[lxxviii]

Wall of an ancient church. (Giuseppe Maio)

THE NEBULOUS YEARS

In the 1200's, a document from Sulmona, Abbruzzi, dated September 2, 1275 sheds light on who ruled the area. This document ...offers a list of various feudal lords and an accurate picture of the Calabrian nobility of those times."[lxxix] The fourth lord listed in the document is Giovanni di Rocca (Giovanni from Rocca), as the possessor of a location in the Rocca territory, named "Ammirato." This location had been given to him by the King, on January 16, 1266.

In the same catalogue, other people are mentioned who also owned lands within the Rocca territory, such as Raimondo di Contissa, Rogerio Caracza, Palmerio Picinna and Agnesia, daughter of Rainaldo Senice.[lxxx]

According to the calculations done by Giuseppe Pardi, in 1921, based on the records of taxation of the time, in 1276, the population of Rocca Niceforo was 1228.[lxxxi] According to Pardi, the population of my village that same year was 343. Nearby, Castel Monardo had a population of 783; Vallelonga had reached a population of 1371.[lxxxii]

In the *Acta Imperii* of 1206, it is confirmed that two hamlets in the territory of Rocca Niceforo were given to Guido di Chiaromonte, by the King of Sicily, because of his devotion and services that he had demonstrated toward the ruler.[lxxxiii]

THE BLESSED NORMAN PERIOD

The Norman period was one of the most positive times for the area. The Normans, led by Roger and Robert Hauteville, made it their task to free Southern Italy from the Saracen scourge. After freeing Palermo, on January 10, 1072, Robert left the conquest of the rest of Sicily to his brother, which he accomplished thanks to his highly mobile army.[lxxxiv] He defeated the brutal Saracens, and delivered Calabria from their scourge.

As the Byzantines before them, they too recognized the strategic importance of the fortress, and Count Roger (Ruggero), as we are informed by Count Roger's biographer and great admirer, the Benedectine monk, Geoffrey (Goffredo) Malaterra, fortified it with towers and bastions.[lxxxv] "He, in truth, strengthened, with the utmost care, with towers and bastions the fortress named Nicefora and provided it with armed soldiers."[lxxxvi] In time, Roger turned the fortress into a critical bastion of defense. In the year 1130, with the formation of the Regnum Siciliae, (The beautiful Kingdom), as was referred to by some historians, "...a new era began, an era of fervor, of peace and of work."[lxxxvii]

Historian Giuseppe Greco describes the period as follows:

> The Normans gave to Southern Italy an atmosphere of serenity and of peace, after the scary nightmares unleashed by the Saracens. On the lands of Calabria rose a dawn of awakening, of enthusiasm, of activity.

The cities started re-flourishing in the arts and in wealth. Churches and castles rose, among which was the one known as Rocca Niceforo, and around the castles rose the hamlets which had been destroyed by the Saracens.[lxxxviii]

It is during this time that the Calabrian Church which previously was directed by the Eastern Church, moved under the control of the Roman Church. Tithes (ten percent of one's income), were paid to the new spiritual overseer. The tithe was divided into four parts. One part went to the Bishop, one part went to the clerics, one part went to the poor, and one part was assigned to the building of churches.[lxxxix]

The preceding period revolved around the arrival of perhaps the most cruel invaders ever to step on Calabrian soil: The Saracens. This was a period of great anxiety, not only for the people of the Rocca, but for all of Calabria and many parts of Southern Italy.

Section of a protective wall. *(Giuseppe Maio)*

Ruins of an ancient building. *(Giuseppe Maio)*

9. THE SARACENS: THE DEMONS FROM AFRICA

A round the year 800 A.D., Sicily had been overrun by Saracens, a fierce North-African tribe bent on conquest and expansion. Once the island had been conquered, they were ready to attempt an invasion of Calabria, the toe of the Italian peninsula, as a precursor to an invasion of all of Southern Italy.

With unparalleled persistence, they captured Calabrian centers, like the formidable fortress of Santa Severina, on the Sila Mountains, and other cities on the western side of Calabria, such as Tropea and Amantea, both not very far from my area.

My people lived just about one hundred kilometers north of the straight of Messina. Day-time, or night-time incursions were easy, since they had settled in an area where the high rocky, almost unconquerable cliffs of Southern Calabria ended and the undefended, easily accessible beaches began. In fact, the mouth of the Angitola River would have offered a perfect spot where small ships could go inland and where the Saracens could land without the interference of high waves.

My ancestors' only protection was the fortress on the nearby mountain on the south side of the Angitola River. But the attacks were frequent and sudden. The anxiety and horror of the brutal and horrifying-looking Saracens drove many to move inland to various locations east of the coast. These small groups were the origins of the people who gave rise to the towns of Maierato, Filogaso, San Nicola, Capistrano, Monte Rosso, Francavilla and Castel Monardo.

But many other courageous souls would not move away from the safety of the fortress. The stunning beauty of the Mediterranean, the rich soil, the fish-rich sea and river were hard to leave behind.

In the meantime, my village and the various other hamlets of the area developed and grew. The land proved ideal for olive groves, vines and fruit trees. The strong, rugged people cut terraces into the sides of the hills, and found the land to be ideal for growing vegetables as well. The plateau on the mountain behind the town was perfect for wheat. Forests abounded all around. The future bode well for them–or so they thought. In reality, future events would have dashed their hopes and dreams in the not-so-distant future.

The whole area was about to face one of the most dangerous periods they had ever faced. The Saracens, the unstoppable Moslem predators from the sea, were readying to bring their brand of horror to all of Calabria, and to my area in particular.

The year 950, the Saracens finally unleashed their fury on the Rocca Fortress. They surrounded its high walls and, after an unknown period of time, they were somehow able to poison the fortress' drinking water, and were finally able to conquer it.[xc] Some inhabitants of the Rocca escaped; others were killed or taken as slaves.

The Saracens went on to also attack the eighteen hamlets dependent on the Rocca, in the nearby valleys, which were not fortified. They killed, maimed, and then kidnapped as many people as they could.

Historian, Giovanni Manfrida, explains that the Saracen attacks were started by the Emir Hasan with help of the African Caliph, Farhang Mahaddet. They were meant to punish Calabrian cities for not having paid their tribute and because of the news that Emperor Constantine Porphirogenitus was planning an attack against them.

Manfrida also adds that during this expedition, the village of Capistrano was taken; many inhabitants were killed; young men were taken to be sold as slaves, and the young women for their harems.[xci]

Once the destruction was almost complete, and the lucrative young men and women were captured, they chained them and forced them to walk toward the coast. Down they stumbled inside the rugged, stony path of the stream that flowed toward the sea. And then the grueling walk down the valley; the incomprehensible commands; the pushing and punching; the stumbling and falling; the agonizing pain on the bare-naked feet; the horror…

After the seemingly never-ending trek, they approached the edge of the mountain where the Fortress was located. One more hope: maybe the Rocca people would have come to their rescue. They looked at the Rocca from the distance and hoped. Unfortunately, as they approached, it became painfully clear that the Fortress had also been attacked and conquered, and that many of its inhabitants may have also been captured and, like them, may have been taken as slaves.

By now their anguish must have been multiplied by the thought that their relatives and friends who had chosen to stay behind in the Rocca may have been killed, or may have been taken as well. In fact, that event was a holocaust for my people, since, not only was my village and the Rocca attacked, but, as already mentioned, seventeen other hamlets and villages which had been begotten by the people of the Rocca had been attacked as well. Both the mother, and its children had been violated by the brutal invaders. The year 950 would have become an unforgettable year of darkness for them and their descendents.

Without doubt, some distraught parents followed from the distance, hiding behind bushes and trees, as their beloved sons and daughters were being forcefully taken away. From their hiding places, they could behold the crowded beaches, and their children being forced onto small, menacing ships. They looked on the agonizing spectacle… speechless. They heard the last screams of horror. They may have witnessed the last agonizing struggles and the last abuses. Then the powerful sails rose, and the ships slowly crawled out to sea, and moved south toward Tropea, Sicily or Africa. Gradually, they disappeared in the cruel horizon…

Though they killed, plundered and destroyed everything they could, if my coin was there, it was not taken. Perhaps a child held it tightly into his hands, as tears were streaming down his cheeks.

Perhaps the parents had been taken away, and the coin was a precious, comforting possession the child hung on to, in all the horrifying chaos. Perhaps someone may have hidden it well, and it remained with the possessor. If the coin was there, it was one treasure the Saracens were not able to take.

SEEKING SAFER HAVENS

As a result of the tragic events described above, many survivors from the Rocca Fortress, and some from the nearby village of Montesanto, moved to Capistrano to seek refuge, only to find that the town had been destroyed.[xcii]

The realization that the village was no longer a safe haven may have pushed the surviving inhabitants and the new arrivals to seek the security of higher grounds. There is a Capistrano tradition that before the people had finally settled on the side of Mount Coppari they had lived on the flat area atop the adjacent mountain. Perhaps this is what the tradition refers to. No archeological remains have been found that an actual stone village existed on that location. This may have been due to their brief stay, and the fact that they had no intention of building stone houses, given more possible attacks.

Another possibility is that only part of the population moved to higher grounds, and others remained below. Perhaps a third possibility may be true as well: They may have worked their fruitful lands below, during the day, and may have walked back up to the mountain in the evening where they would have been safer through the night.

In fact, the tenuousness of their situation may have been further reinforced by a probable, second attack which may have occurred thirty-three years later, when the coast was again plundered, and the nearby city of Bivona (today's Vibo Valentia), was "totally razed to the ground" by the Saracens, and was not re-built for two hundred years.[xciii]

By this point, the people of my village had to come up with a long term solution. Being in the proximity of the Angitola River and given the fact that the coast was no longer safe. They had to move further away to a much safer location. The village of Vallelonga would have been the ideal location. It was positioned on higher grounds, and further away from the coast than Capistrano. There, the powerful count of Arena, Lord of the area, and of the local castle, might have offered them protection.

Thus, many asked the Count for protection. Their request was granted, and they became his servants working his land in exchange for the basics and, most of all, in exchange for protection. A few courageous souls, though, refused to leave their lands, and stayed behind.[xciv]

The others served the Arena family from 1122 to 1304. Once the Saracen danger had greatly diminished, they longed to return to their lands. Their request was granted, and they returned to their beloved village, once again

From Capistrano, looking toward the Angitola Mountain, and the Mediterranean. The Saracens trudged up this valley to the village of Capistrano to kidnap and destroy. The Rocca Fortress was located on the distant mountain. The ships waited where the mountain inclines toward the Mediterranean Sea, to carry the youth away to distant lands to sell them into slavery. The same brutality was repeated several times all over Calabria. (M. Caputo)

10. HOW MUCH SARACEN BLOOD IS THERE IN CALABRIANS?

ome Italians, and some North Americans have asserted that we Calabrians are "Moors," that is Africans. In saying so, they erroneously assume that in the past all of Calabria was conquered by the African Saracens, and that they remained in Calabria in large numbers, after their defeat by the Normans.

Furthermore, some erroneously assume that the history of Calabria is essentially the same as that of Sicily, which was, indeed, conquered totally by the Saracens who ruled over it for about two hundred years and where *some* Arabs remained after their defeat. Calabria's experience with the Saracens was quite different. Although some cities were conquered, and controlled *temporarily*, the Saracens never succeeded in conquering the whole Region, and colonizing it, as they did in Sicily.

As stated above, some areas were conquered by the Saracens, such as Reggio, in the southernmost part of Calabria; Tropea, Amantea and the Rocca Fortress, on the south-western side; Squillace, Santa Severina, and Catanzaro on the Central-Eastern side and Cosenza, and Rossano on the northern side.

Reggio was conquered by the Saracens in 902. This conquest lasted a few months, and a new conquest was attempted again in

918, after which they forced the people to pay 22.000 nomismata, yearly, which was later halfed by the year 924. By 934, Reggio stopped the payment. In 951 the Saracens crossed the straight and conquered Reggio, and forced them to pay again. In 978-981 Reggio and other centres were sacked again. Finally, all attacks ceased in 1031, with the advent of a civil war in Sicily.[xcv]

In 906 they took Catanzaro, by night, and after having butchered part of the population, they took the rest to nearby Squillace as slaves. They, of course plundered all their possessions as well.[xcvi] In spite of the seemingly hopeless state of affairs, Calabrians did not take the invasions lying down. In the some areas, they revolted, and fought the invaders bravel.

In 921 a rebellion by Calabrians forced the Saracens to leave Calabria. The following year, a determined Saracen leader by the name of Mikael (Asklabio), returned with fury, and sacked and destroyed anywhere he could. This continued until 934 when again the Calabrians revolted fiercely, and the Saracens were conclusively forced to leave[xcvii]

But the invasions did not end. Calabrians were in a state of ongoing fear, for a long time still. The saracens could appear at any time, unannounced, to pillage, destroy, and take young Calabrians away as slaves, until they were finally defeated by Catholic forces, and pushed back to Africa.

Therefore, the assertion that Calabrians are in large part "Moors" is unfounded. The Saracens used Calabria as an area to pillage, and to take young people away as slaves. They did not settle there as a people, nor did they create large colonies as they did in Sicily. The reason was simple: Their people would have been in danger by the Byzantines who ruled *most* of Calabria, by the Normans that followed them, and by angry locals who did not take invasions by non-Christians as acceptable, and rebelled whenever they could.

Historian, Augusto Placanica synthesizes the struggle between the Saracens, and the Byzantines in Calabria in the following statement: "Calabria...was a systematic battlefield...in the mortal challenge between the Arabs and the Eastern Empire."[xcviii]

The Calabrian areas that were temporarily conquered were simply Arab military "arrowheads" into enemy territory; they were strategic locations from where future expansions were to take place. Some places, like Tropea, Amantea and Rocca Angitola became simply military fortresses kept for strategic purposes.

Calabrians' response to the Saracen arrival was to simply move inland, which is the main reason why countless villages were created on the mountainous regions, away from the coast.

Carmelo Martorana, a 19th-century Sicilian historian who saw the Saracens as part of his ancestry, and who held them in the highest esteem, wrote the following about the Saracens' attitude toward Calabria, in particular, and toward the rest of Italy, in general.

> (After having subjugated Sicily, the Saracens) ...put forth such strength, that the riches of the Italic territory and its

peoples waited for two centuries as prepared prey of the Sicilian Saracens as a meal specifically destined to fatten those our peoples. Thus the Sicilian Emirs invested ever-increasing concern to denuding that land with incursions and thefts instead of subjugating them with sieges and with judiciously prepared battles. Furthermore the Arab historians especially praise the Sicilian governors, for having enriched the nation (Sicily) and filled the treasury with ransacking and the tributes they oppressed Calabrians with.[xcix]

The Saracens, therefore, proved to be more interested in sporadic pillaging than conquering; pillaging that went on for decades, which impoverished the Calabrians, and enriched the Sicilian Saracens.

In spite of the relentless incursions, Calabria stood firm against the brutal Saracens. The Orthodox Byzantines, the Catholic Normans, and the fiery Calabrians, created a barrier the Saracens tried to totally penetrate in vain. Finally, they were pushed back into their ships, and were forced to go back to where they originated from.

11. THE CHILDREN OF THE ANGITOLA FORTRESS

THE "LIVING" CHILDREN

The following towns are populated by the descendents of families that over the centuries moved inland from the Rocca Angitola to the hills adjacent to the Angitola Valley.

FRANCAVILLA *(Google Earth)*

MONTEROSSO CALABRO *(Paul August)*

Michael Caputo

SAN NICOLA DA CRISSA *(Mack1970)*

MAIERATO *(M. Caputo)*

FILOGASO *(Google Earth)*

THE "NO-LONGER-LIVING" CHILDREN OF THE ROCCA ANGITOLA

The following were productive hamlets and villages for centuries. They are now totally deserted.

NICASTRELLO: *Presently, part of Capistrano's territory, but uninhabited, as of a few decades ago. (M. Caputo)*

MONTESANTO: *Chiesa Dell'Assunzione. (C. La Serra)*

PIMENE: *Santa Maria delle Grazie Church. (C. La Serra)*

PRONIA: *Little is left of this village anciently found in this general area. (C. La Serra)*

PANAJA: *Anciently located on this hill, found next to the town of Filogaso. (C. La Serra)*

Ruin of the Rocca with the Angitola Lake in the background. Capistrano is one of the towns nestled on the side of the Mountain, in the distance. The other towns of the Angitola Valley are located on hills on both sides of the lake. (Giuseppe Maio)

The Angitola Lake, as seen from the south end.(M. Caputo)

12. FILADELFIA: A CALABRIAN UTOPIA

Filadelfia is not a direct descendent of the Rocca Angitola. Its people find their roots in the city of Castel Monardo located very near the Rocca. Before the year 850 AD, its people moved inland from the coast. Without doubt, many or most came from the area of the Scrisi Plain adjacent to the Rocca. In time, some of the inhabitants of the Rocca moved into the safe walls of Castel Monardo, just a few Kilometers inland, to escape the Muslim fury. When the city was destroyed by the 1783 earthquakes, the resilient and courageous people of Castel Monardo created the very beautiful Filadelfia, located just a few kilometers from the Rocca Fortress. This is its amazing story.

A few years ago, I got to know a friendly young science teacher in my high school with an Irish name and Mediterranean looking features. He explained to me that the reason his name was Irish was because his father was Irish Canadian, while his Mediterranean features came from his mom who, he told me, came from Southern Italy. I asked the young man where she came from exactly and, wonder of wonders, it came out that she came from a small city only about 10 Kilometers from mine; a city I heard about but that, unfortunately, I had never visited.

Over time, Greg shared some very interesting, and intriguing details about his mom's city that led me to want to research it further, so as to get the whole story, since Greg did not know all the important details.

Greg told me that the people from his mom's city originated from a town which had been destroyed long ago by an earthquake, and which had never been rebuilt. He also vaguely mentioned a Bishop that apparently had led the reconstruction not too far away from the original town.

So I started digging into Greg's past, using Italian historical sources, mostly to give him a deeper knowledge of his roots. Amazingly, in so doing, I came across a most fascinating story.

Greg was right: his ancestors had come from another town. That town's name was Castel Monardo (Monardo Castle) and, indeed, it had been destroyed, not by one but *several* very powerful earthquakes, in 1783. In fact, I also found that that same town had also been destroyed by other powerful quakes in 1638 and in 1659.

In 1783, one of their egregious sons, Bishop Giovanni Andrea Serrao, a very well known, and highly respected Bishop in the Catholic Church who belonged to a rich and highly respected family, proposed to the traumatized people that it was time to move away from the area, and build another city from scratch.

Not far away, closer to the sea, there was a mountain with a relatively flat area at the top, with fertile lands all around. The few buildings in that area had been damaged somewhat by the earthquakes, but they had not been destroyed. That area would have been the location where they would have finally found peace and relative safety.

Bishop Serrao was supported in this quest by his six brothers who also belonged to the nobility, and who were deeply respected by their people.

The people of the area referred to the horrifying time as "The Scourge,"[c] that is, the great punishment from God, and the reason they concluded that was because they recognized that they had been sinners and uncaring toward one another.

The inhabitants were ready to listen, and gladly followed the direction of the Bishop whom they loved and respected.

Ruins of Castel Monardo. (M. Caputo)

Bishop Serrao, a visionary man and a true leader, went on to propose that they not only build a new city in a new area, but that they build a new city built on Christian values and morals; a city that would have been a shining example of true Christianity to all the other cities and towns all around.

Indeed, the new city would have been exceptional, because of its revolutionary city planning, and architecture but, most of all, because it would have been a city built on Christian love. In fact, he proposed a beautiful name which was to be the mission statement for the people of old Castel Monardo: the City of Filadelfia; that is "The City of Brotherly Love." The aim of the new society was to teach its inhabitants, "To learn ...to love their friends and brothers and to have the same love toward all men."[ci]

The people felt greatly inspired by the Bishop's vision, and they quickly went to work to build this new and amazing city. The money to rebuild came from the government, the Serrao family and other rich families. The people would freely offer their labor as well.

The design was to be perfectly geometric. The streets would have been larger than any other city in the area. The main streets would have been avenues. In the middle of the city there would have been a large and beautiful square, and around the square four large churches.

Bishop Serrao led the way, not only financially, but with his example. A document of the time describes him as having "...tenderly loved his town," and as having "...loved all the citizens of this city as his beloved brethren." He also, "...financed schools which among other things taught morals and principles that would make his fellow citizens wiser, good and better Christians."[cii]

Love was to be the glue that would have kept the city together;

love would have been the spirit that would have characterized the dealings of the people toward each other, and love was what characterized the leader, Bishop Serrao, who set the example in every way.

The utopia worked for quite some time. The people lived in harmony for years. Then something tragic happened.

Bishop Serrao had been sent by the Pope to oversee an area in another part of Italy. The Bishop was known to support democratic ideals; he was known not to support the church hierarchy. Furthermore, he was also known to want to empower the people, and give them more of a say in government. He had enemies– enemies that wanted him gone.

On a tragic day, his enemies organized an uprising. A large group of mercenaries captured the Bishop, killed him, chopped his head off, and then callously paraded his head through the city.

When the news reached Filadelfia, the city was traumatized. Not only was the head of the Bishop cut off, so was the head of the new vision named Filadelfia. Bishop Serrao's brothers were fine people, and they were very respected as well; but the people's greatest source of inspiration was Bishop Serrao–and he was gone.

In time the Bishop's brothers died as well, and the new leaders were more interested in themselves that in maintaining a utopian vision. Gradually the vision came to an end. Filadelfia retained its geometric shape, its wide avenues, its impressive buildings, but, in time, it lost its utopian spirit, and the spirit of love was replaced with the same competitive spirit that characterized all the surrounding cities and towns.

In the Summer of 2010, I was in the area to visit my family and, while there, I went to visit the ruins of Castel Monardo and the beautiful little city of Filadelfia. I spent almost a whole day in the area. I took a large number of pictures, and spoke to some local, knowledgeable people. One of them knew the history of the area exceptionally well. He shared fascinating details about both cities, and did so with enthusiasm.

I left the city filled with wonderment at what my Calabrian brothers in the area had experienced, and what they had accomplished. I left more than ever amazed with Filadelfia's beloved son, Andrea Serrao, who did so much for his people, and who had many more honorable plans for the people of Italy, but was unable to bring them to fruition.

But Filadelfia's idealistic past did not just fizzle and die. As later historical events clearly indicate, the people of this amazing, small city again showed their courage, and their longing for a better world by volunteering in unusually large numbers to fight on Garibaldi's side as he fought against the Spanish Bourbons, to help create a united Italy, free from foreign oppression.

It is because of this legacy that in 1906, when the King of Italy went to visit the many areas of Calabria which had been affected by a cataclysmic earthquake, he asked to visit Filadelfia, even though the damage to the city had been minimal. The real reason for his request was to honor the birthplace of the large number of Filadelfian heroes who had fought for the unification of Italy,

A visit to Filadelfia ought to be a must for anyone who visits Central Calabria. I also recommend a visit to the adjacent, ghost town of Castel Monardo, devastated by the 1783 earthquakes. The great damage one can witness is indicative of what befell a great many Calabrian towns during that catastrophic period.

Filadelfia's Main Square. (M. Caputo)

One of the several palazzos built by Filadelfians. (M. Caputo)

Facade of one of four churches located around Filadelfia's main square.(M. Caputo)

13. THE BYZANTINES: MORE GREEK-SPEAKING IMMIGRANTS ARRIVE IN CALABRIA

This phase in Calabria's history is considered by some historians to have been a dark period. What is known about it is based on rare imperial edicts and ecclesiastical documents. "These are the only elements that allow us to look into and and observe closely into the social and economic life of the calabria of the times."[ciii]

The Byzantines remained in Calabria for about five hundred years, often in competition with the Longobards who had deprived them of the control over the peninsula. Because of ongoing wars, Northern Calabria was alternatively, and at times simultaneously, under the control of both powers.

The Byzantines burdened Calabria with heavy taxes, but "...made the region a centre of civilization which was continually enriched by the arrival of refugees who had escaped from the territories conquered by the Arabs (from the Orient and North Africa)."[civ]

It was during this period that monks who were escaping the Muslim fury moved into Calabria carrying with them precious ancient books, culture and knowledge.[cv] One such group was responsible for the creation of the convent of Santa Maria, in my area. Another such convent was created just a few kilometers north of my village, known as Sant'Elia.

It was during the VIII century that the land which had been known as Bruzio began to be called, Calabria, a name which, previously, referred mostly to the area of the Puglie Region.

During the Byzantine rule, the Saracens captured the Rocca Fortress and controlled it for a few decades.

Around the year 885, the city was liberated by the Byzantine general, Niceforo Foca, who had been sent to Italy by Emperor Basilius I, with a strong army to fight the Saracens. As a result of having defeated the Saracens, the Rocca was named Rocca Niceforo, a name that it retained for centuries.

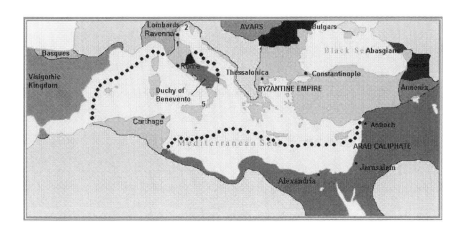

The Byzantine Empire by 650 A.D. Calabria was under the control of the Eastern Empire. Unfortunately, much pressure would soon follow, due to the fast-expanding and fierce Muslim hordes. (Map by, Justinian43)

La Cattolica di Stilo: A very famous church built in the Basilian-Byzantine style in Stilo, Southern Calabria. It is one of Calabria's seven UN World heritage sites.(Saverio Rutellitano)

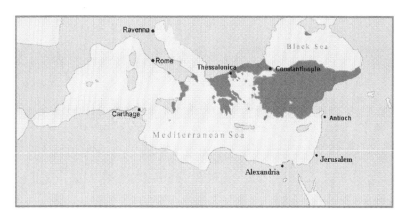

The Byzantine Empire (867 A.D.). Due to pressures from all sides, the Byzantine Empire had decreased significantly in size. Calabria was to remain under its control until the new millenium.
(Bigdaddy1204)

14. THE MIGHTY ROMANS CONQUER CALABRIA

The Angitola Fortress was an important way station during Roman times. It was located beside the Via Popilia, a very important road used by the Romans to quickly transfer troops to any area in Calabria and Sicily to quell any uprising. In time, it became important for commercial purposes as well.

Dr. Greco found references to the Fortress in the Roman Emperor, Antoninus Pius' work, "Itinerary." Emperor Antoninus wrote that the Fortress was a way station of the major Roman Road named, Via Popilia. According to Greco, in ancient Roman times the fortress was called, "Crissa."

> During Roman times, as remembered in the "Itinerary" of Emperor Antoninus Pius, it was a "Mansio," that is a way station of the Via Popilia. In Crissa the travelers could stop to spend the night and get restored. There, the couriers, would exchange their exhausted horses. We are in an obligatory location, where the city would dominated the life of the low and upper Calabria. It, therefore, from its beginning, had the character of a fortress and remained such over time.[cvi]

We do no know how large the population had become by Roman times. The Romans had clearly made the fortress a major stop for the couriers who were regularly traveling south to, or north from the major colonies in Southern Calabria. The Via Popilia was the only thoroughfare which traversed Calabria in those days, and the fortress would have become a relatively prosperous location, thanks to the many people who traveled north or south. The land was also very fruitful, and the farmers could have abundantly provided for themselves, and for the travelers who passed by.

The above information was very interesting, but the most interesting detail was that the ancient name of the fortress was, "Crissa." Why Crissa? Dr. Greco did not help with the meaning of the name, but he definitely helped with the evolving events since Roman times.

In his work, *Rocca Angitola*, he informs us that the area was attacked by Barbarians. "With the crumbling of the Roman Empire, Crissa followed the destiny of all of Calabria, on which the Heruli, the Goths...had an impact."[cvii] How much destruction did these barbaric people bring on the area? They clearly were in the area not to civilize but to pillage; not to bring, but to take. Did they attack the Rocca? Being an important fortress, it probably was. Was there any resistance? Again, we can only surmise that the Roman soldiers might have put up a valiant fight. The fearful area inhabitants may have fled the barbarian invaders, and probably hid in nearby forests, or may have moved away to the nearby mountains.

But it was not the barbarians' plan to stay. They ravaged the area, and left. Fortunately, as discussed above, a more benevolent master followed them; a master they had much in common with: the Greek-speaking Byzantine Emperor.

FROM HIPPONION TO HIPPONIUM TO VALENTIA

The city of Hipponion (today's Vibo Valentia, the capital city of my area of Calabria), located on the west coast of Calabria, about 15 Kilometers from my town, was a major Greek colony founded by the Locrians.[cviii] This took place the seventh century, decades after they had arrived from Greece, and had settled in Locri Epizephyrii.[cix]

Hipponion had been a very prosperous Greek colony, until the middle of the third century before Christ, when it was conquered by a people who had populated the mountainous regions of Calabria, after coming down from Central Italy, called the "Bretti" or "Brutii" (Bruzi, in Italian).

These people had moved into Italy over three thousand years ago, probably from Illyria, on the Adriatic side and, over the centuries, moved to Southern Italy. In their quest for expansion, they conquered Hipponion, and ruled over it for a few decades, until they were attacked, and defeated by a much more powerful expansionistic power, the Romans, who gave the colony a Latin name: "Hipponium" and later "Valentia."

Hipponium was a major control centre for the Romans, and large numbers of soldiers were stationed there to protect the strategically vital harbor, nearby. During the war between Octavian (later, Augustus Caesar) and Pompeus, the future Emperor made the city his headquarters from which he directed the entire war against his opponent. [cx]

The port nearby must have been a major centre for ships traveling to Africa and other Mediterranean locations. The Apostle Paul saw the mountain on his way to Puteoli, after leaving Rhegium, but the ship did not stop.[cxi]

Were slaves brought to Hipponium to assist the rich Romans who controlled the commerce in the area? No doubt some were. How many? We do not know. Some of them and their offspring must have stayed in the area, and must have intermarried with the locals. Where were they from? It could have been any part of the Empire.

JEWS IN CALABRIA?

Jews were brought to Italy, after the conquest of Judea, during the first and second century after Christ. Some were brought as slaves to Southern Italy. After the fall of the Roman Empire, others followed, as freemen, for commercial purposes. According to some sources, in those days, some Calabrian centers were half Jewish. Some Jews lived in the nearby plain city of St. Eufemia, and Hipponium which became a prosperous commercial centre. Jews became prosperous merchants in that city, until their expulsion.[cxii]

According to the *Historical Archives of the Neapolitan Provinces*, some Jews were actually living in Pizzo Calabro, and in the Rocca Fortress, before their expulsion. In 1541 all Jews were totally expelled from the southern Kingdom, by the ruling Spaniards, unless they converted to Catholicism.[cxiii] Some may have converted; some may have intermarried; a few may have stayed in the Rocca, and surrounding areas, and intermarried later. Exact numbers are unknown.

We know that some Jews are still in Calabria today. Are they the descendents of the Jews who stayed behind centuries ago? Hard to say. We might speculate that at least a few might be, while others may have come to Calabria later for various reasons.

The Italian-Jewish Rabbi, Barbara Aiello, is presently trying to gather Calabrian Jews. A synagogue was recently opened in the town of Serrastretta, in Central Calabria, so as to serve them.[cxiv]

FROM GREEK TO LATIN

The conquering Romans were in no hurry to erase the Greek civilization they ruled over. They learned from it; they absorbed it; perhaps, because of the supreme achievements of the ancient Greeks in all areas of endeavor, they gladly allowed Greece to culturally conquer them. Linguistically, it's hard to say to what extent my area had been Latinized. Some believe the latinization was total; others do not hold the same view.

Perhaps the answer lies between the two contrasting views. The major centers, such as Hipponium, were quickly Latinized, due to the fact that the majority of inhabitants originated from Central Italy. Other areas away from Hipponium, such as Napitia

(Pizzo), and Crissa may have been only partially Latinized. Farming communities, farther away from the major colonies, may have remained mostly Greek-speaking. It may be safe to assume that in most of Calabria a mongrel language, part Greek, part Latin may have evolved over time.

This, of course was temporary, as the Calabrian population moved totally back to Greek, once the Greek-Byzantines took over in the sixth century A.D., and retained the area for about 500 years, until the 11th century A.D.

Roman Mosaic. Archeological park, S. Aloe, in Vibo Valentia.
(Manuel zinnà2)

15. THE ANCIENT GREEKS DISCOVER CALABRIA

T he next question that needed answering was, what was the history of my people before the Romans? This was another fascinating layer I needed to explore, in detail.

In ancient times, Southern Italy had been named, "Megálē Hellás" by the Greeks, and "Magna Grecia" by the Latins. The latter term is still used, on occasion, by cultured Italians, when referring to Southern Italy. The term has been given two different meanings since ancient times; one referring to Southern Italy being "greater" than Greece, in terms of accomplishments, and one referring to the fact that the territory was simply "larger" than the motherland. This debate even today "...has not landed to a definitive conclusion."[cxv]

I had known, vaguely, that in ancient times Greeks had colonized the coastal areas. What I did not know was how extensive the colonization had been, and the fact that my area of Calabria had also welcomed a very large number of Greeks. In fact, a large number moved to Calabria during the sixth, and seventh centuries before Christ, and that many more joined them during the period of the Byzantine Empire, from around 500 to 1000 A.D.

Over the centuries, the Greeks created many colonies. They poured into Southern Italy from various parts of Greece, like a seemingly endless river. All, or most of the great Greek city states, had sent colonizers to Italy, and the results were a Hellenized Southern Italy. Thus, Sparta colonized Tarentum; Achaia created the colonies of Metapontum, Sybaris and Kroton; Colophon founded Siris; Thuri belonged to Athens; the Locrians founded Locri Epizephyrii; Chalcis colonized Cumae; the Phocians, founded Elea; Chalcis, created Rhegion.[cxvi]

Magna Grecia became the birthplace of several famous Greeks, though very few today know about this. The great Greek scientist, Archimedes, for instance, was born in the Greek colony of Syracuse, in south-eastern Sicily. Zeno of Elea, the ancient philosopher who according to Aristotle invented the Dialectic, was born in the Greek colony of Elea. Zaleucus the lawgiver, who was responsible for the first written laws in Europe, was a native son of Locri Epizephyrii. Timeus of Locri was a philosopher of such note that Plato dedicated a whole "Dialogue" to him. According to Plato, Timeus had achieved, "...the greatest honor in philosophy."[cxvii] Pythagoras moved to Kroton in Calabria to found a society that became both a religious community, and a scientific school.[cxviii]

Many great Greek athletes came from Magna Grecia as well. The city of Kroton produced many of the greatest athletes in the ancient Greek world. In fact, Milo of Kroton was one of the greatest wrestlers in the ancient world. He wore the Olympian crown six times in wrestling.[cxix] Euthymus of Locri, from Locri Epizephyrii, was the three-time winner in the boxing event in

Olympia (484, 476 and 472 B.C.).[cxx]

These were just some of the famed Italian-Greeks who excelled yearly in the city of Olympia.

Greek Temple of Hera, located in Selinunte, Sicily. One of several Greek temples found in Southern Italy. (AdiJapan)

CALABRIA: FIRST TO BE CALLED "ITALIA"

I do not recall if I was already aware of this detail or not, but, most probably on my first visit to the Vatican Museum, while observing the gigantic ancient maps found on the walls of the stunning, "Hall of Maps," I saw something which would leave many quite surprised. While reading the names of the various areas of Italy before Christ, I was amazed to notice that in the ancient past there was only one area in the whole Italian peninsula named

"Italia," and that area was Calabria.

This detail would leave many astounded, and others, who don't particularly like Calabrians, upset. How can the poorest region in Italy have given such glorious name to the nation? Though surprising, it is indeed an undeniable fact: Calabria was the very first area in Italy to be named "Italia," and it is from Calabria that the name poured northward into the rest of Italy.

But what did Italia mean? T wo possibilities are offered by historians: one very flattering, the second not so flattering.

According to Virgil, in his third book of the Aeneid and Thucydides, Calabria was named "Italia" after Italus, a just and loved ruler of the area, 7-8 centuries before Christ. [cxxi]

Others see no such connection, and simply see its roots in the Oscan word "Vitelii" meaning land of bulls or calves. [cxxii]

Whatever the original meaning of the now world-renowned name, "Italia," Calabrians can be proud of one thing no one can take away from them: the name "Italia" began in their beloved Region.

Beside its most famous name, in ancient times Calabria was named by various other names as well. The other names were Bruttium, Saturnia, Ausonia, Enotria, Tirrenia, and Esperia. [cxxiii]

GREEKS—BUT FROM WHERE?

But who were the Greeks who had moved to my area? Where had they come from? I was compelled to find the origins of these people as well.

The search in time proved quite fruitful. The history of the Greeks in my area had been studied quite thoroughly. They were Greek people who had emigrated from the eastern side of Calabria, during the seventh century B.C. As explained above, they had moved to Hipponion from the ancient city of Locri Epizephyrii, near the present and prosperous Calabrian city of Locri, on the south-east side of Calabria.

Locri had been founded by colonizing Greeks, during the seventh century B.C.[cxxiv] and quickly became a prosperous and strong city. Its people had emigrated to Calabria from central Greece looking for fertile lands, and they found them in Calabria.

The coast was beautiful; the mountains nearby abounded in wood, and water poured down the valleys in large quantities. On that shimmering coast, they would have had great quantities of fish. On the coastal lands, fruit trees would have produced in great abundance. The nearby hills would have been ideal for their precious olive trees and their grape vines.

Upon their arrival, they had settled about twenty-five kilometers south of Locri. This was a port known to the Greeks as they had used it for trading purposes or for replenishing their boats, as they traveled north from the southernmost part of Calabria. The area was populated by indigenous people called, "Siculi," who had arrived much earlier from central Italy[cxxv] and quickly made a pact of mutual co-operation with them.

Polibius informs us that the Greek newcomers acted

treacherously, tricked the locals and finally suppressed them, after their defeat. [cxxvi]

Upon exploring the northern coast, it was concluded that the area twenty-five kilometers north of their first place of arrival would have been a better location where to create a new city, because of more fertile soil and more abundant water; and thus they moved. This occurred according to Eusebius in 673. Others push the date back about two decades. [cxxvii] The name, "Locri," was a way of remembering their state of origin in Greece. "Zephyrii" had been added in the original colony as a term descriptive of the harbor where they originally landed. The promontory adjacent to the harbor protected the area from the "Zephyr" wind and thus the added descriptor. When the Locrians moved north and created their new colony they retained the name. [cxxviii]

The great Greek geographer of ancient times, Strabo, refers to Locri Epizephyrii in his geographic masterwork, *Geographica*: "After the promontory of Hercules one finds the one called Lokri Zephir whose harbor is protected by the western winds. Its name derives from this. After it follows the city named Lokri Epizephyrii." [cxxix]

In the meantime, some returned home and announced the news. The new land was naturally rich and could accommodate great numbers; and great numbers came. Hundreds of thousands went to their, "America," and prospered.

FROM EAST TO WEST

The Greek spirit of expansion led the Locrians to want to move on–but to where? The northern side was under the Achaeans who had founded Croton.[cxxx] The south was under the control of the Rhegion Greek colony, founded by Chalcidians from Zancle.[cxxxi] No one controlled the opposite side of Calabria, on the western side, so that became their next goal: To create Locrian colonies in that new promising area.

And so they did. Two colonies were created: Medma and Hipponion.[cxxxii] The two colonies grew quickly and, like the motherland, became strong as well. Most of Southern Calabria was now in Locrian hands.

Locri Epizephyrii. Foundation of ancient building.

Locri Epizephyrii. Remains, and ongoing excavations.

*Magna Grecia. My Greek ancestors moved from Locri Epizephyrii
to the Hipponium area.* (www.satrapa1.com.)

16. BACK TO WARS–JUST LIKE HOME

T he city of Locri grew and became very strong. North of it, the Croton colony became strong as well, and so did Rhegion, south of Locri. They were Greeks as well, but from different states, and that was enough to create competition and later wars, just like back home.

The ancient Greeks were known for their belligerent spirit. Back in Greece, the various states continually fought among themselves. The new land of Calabria was not able to change their nature. The fighting continued there as well.

North of the Locrian territory, the Crotonian Greeks expanded and became prosperous. They were known for their beautiful women, and the athletic prowess their young men.[cxxxiii]

The Croton warriors were confident and capable, and they were thirsty for conquest. They longed to conquer Southern Calabria, but to do so they had to first defeat their Locrian brothers. Thus they amassed a huge army; according to some sources, upwards of 130.000 strong, to attack the southern neighbors.[cxxxiv] The weaker Locrians panicked. Their army was only a fraction of the Crotonians', being only 10 to 15,000 strong.[cxxxv]

They quickly sent messengers to Greece to seek help from the various Greek states, but the mainland Greeks refused to help.

Sparta's help was sought, but they chose not to get involved. The Spartans, according to the ancient historian Diodorus Siculus, instead suggested that the Locrians seek help from the Greek "saving" gods, Castor and Pollux. The Locrians accepted the offer and the statues of the two Greek gods were sent to Locri on a ship.[cxxxvi]

The other Locrians from Medma and Hipponion, on the west coast, joined them.[cxxxvii] The Greeks from Rhegion, just south of Locri, afraid of also being conquered by the Crotonians, allied themselves with the Locrians, and fought on their side as well.[cxxxviii] Given the Crotonian numerical superiority, everything pointed to an inevitable, crushing defeat. In desperation, the southern allies finally decided to use a very risky tactic. They would await the invading army at the Sagra River, north of the city, and allow their cavalry to do most of the work.

CROTON DEFEATED

The exact date of this battle is not known. Historians place the conflict presumably between 560 BC and 535 BC.[cxxxix]

According to legend, the waters of the river turned red, due to the large number of soldiers that were killed. The main reason for the victory appears to have been the wise decision not to wait to confront the Crotonian army at the city walls. They, instead, met them at the Sagra River, in a location located between steep cliffs, and the sea where only a fraction of the Crotonian army could pass through. This allowed the foot soldiers, and the Locrian cavalry to confront only a limited number of Crotonians, instead of the whole army. The ideal location, a valiant cavalry and a desperate, "do-or-die" attitude brought about the demise of the invading Crotonians.[cxl]

But the Locrians did not take the glory. They concluded that the main reason for their victory was the fact that the gods, Castor and Pollux, had been on their side. The legend tells us that during the fierce battle two young men "...wearing scarlet cloaks and mounted on white horses"[cxli] were seen fighting on the side of the Locrian army and were crucial for the decisive victory. They disappeared at the end of the battle.[cxlii]

According to the ancient geographer, Strabo, to express their gratitude, the Locrians dedicated two statues in honor of the Dioscuri brothers (Castor and Pollux), on the edges of the Sagra River.[cxliii]

As a result of this battle, "Locri rose in importance; the power of Croton was broken"[cxliv] The result was also an expansion of Locrian territory north of their area and a shrinking of Crotonian territory. Caulon and Skillion on the East side of Calabria, were taken from the Crotonians. The Crotonians lost territory in the St. Eufemia plains, on the west side of Calabria, as well.[cxlv]

The booty of the battle was great. Some of it was sent to Delphi, to express gratitude to the gods. A shield taken from the Crotonians was found in Delphi, stating that the citizens of Medma, Hipponion and Locri were dedicating it to the gods as a sign of gratitude for their victory. "The Hipponeis dedicated (this spoil taken) from the Crotonians, also the Medmae and the Locrians (dedicated it)."[cxlvi]

The Valley of the Torbido River. The great Battle of the Sagra is presumed to have taken place in this area.(Jacopo)

Capo Colonna, Crotone: The last remaining column of a Greek temple. (Revolweb)

SYBARIS DESTROYED

Croton was humiliated, and it took much time before it would attempt any other conquest. The opportunity finally came in 510 B.C.[cxlvii] The Crotonians welcomed five hundred exiles from the other Achaean colony of Sybaris, which led to a diplomatic debacle, and then war. Thanks to this war, the Crotonians were able to finally fulfill their dream of conquest and expansion.

The attacking army was led by Milon, the famous athlete and a disciple of Pythagoras. Sybaris was defeated, taken and plundered. It was later utterly destroyed. [cxlviii]

Some people see the defeat of Sybaris as a downward cultural turning point for Calabria. Sybaris had been a cultural locomotive, and the locomotive had come to a grinding halt. As John Boardman bemoans, "The destruction of such city may truly be called the end of an epoch."[cxlix]

In 477 B.C., Rhegion entered into a conflict with Locri. The Locrians were joined by Hieron of Syracuse. "From this time, until the mid-fourth century, Locri appears as dependent on Syracuse, particularly on her tyrants."[cl] During the Peloponnesian Wars, Locri, still allied with Syracuse, sent ships to fight Athens in Aegean waters. After the war, Dyonisius the Elder took control of Syracuse and used Locri as his base on Calabrian soil giving rewards to the city for its help in gaining Italian territories.[cli]

Later the city passed between Pyrrhus and the Romans and, later still, during the Punic Wars, it passed between the Romans and the Carthaginians.[clii] In the time of Polybius, "She was still an independent city with pride in the peculiarity of her traditions."[cliii]

FROM CONQUERORS TO CONQUERED

The Locrians had shown their intelligence and their prowess. The three Locrian colonies, Locri, Medma and Hipponion fought together, and flourished together. But, in time, Hipponion and Medma felt ready to become independent city states and they rebelled. This gave rise to a war between Locri, and its two colonies.[cliv] From this point on, the relationship between the mother, and the two daughters was never again the same.

Unfortunately, independence can also lead to weakness. Had all the Greek colonies worked as a unit, it probably would have been impossible for the Bretti (Bruzi) to conquer any Greek colony. But in the third century the Bretti saw their chance, came down from their mountain bases in Northern Calabria, and conquered various southern colonies. The Greek colonies fell, and remained under their control until 194 BC.[clv]

THE INDOMITABLE BRETTI (BRUTII)

The Bretti had slowed down the Roman expansion into Calabria, for decades. They were fierce fighters that valiantly fought and frustrated the Roman armies that had attempted an invasion. The fact that they had overextended themselves to control the various southern Greek colonies may have been a major reason for their weakening.

The Romans saw the Bretti as a frustrating opponent that had to be squashed. In 272 B.C. they sent a large army meant to finish the job once and for all. And so they did. The Bretti were sorely defeated, and dispersed. A large part of their territory was confiscated, and became *Ager Publicus*, that is the property of the Roman people.

The Bretti desperately tried to free themselves from the Romans, during the Second Punic War, by allying themselves with the Carthaginians, but, since the war ended in favour of the Romans, they became servants and slaves. [clvi] Yet, the Bretti blood survives in Calabrians. Perhaps the proverbial Calabrian stubbornness may have some genetic root, in part, in these fierce and stubborn fighters.

The Romans took over all of Calabria, and retained control over it, until the region was taken over by the Byzantine Empire in sixth Century.

THE COIN *WAS NOT* A "SEXTERSIUS"!

While all the historical pieces surrounding my people were being put together, I again had an urge to find more details about my coin. I explored the Internet in depth and found more fascinating facts relating to it. This time the greatest help came from a most distinguished and reliable source: "The British Museum."

The British Museum has a web site that deals specifically with very ancient coins. Coins from Magna Grecia are included. A careful search brought me to coins from Hipponium where, after some careful searching, I found a most well-preserved replica of my coin. Unlike my previous search, this time I also found the details I had craved to find for decades.

According to the British Museum experts, the coin had been minted about 200 years before Christ, in the Roman-Greek colony of Hipponium, while under Roman rule. The undecipherable word on the Cornucopia side of the coin was the word, "Valentia," another name the Romans had given to the city. The "S" on the coin stood for "Semis," as it was half of the main coin minted in the area, somewhat like half of our dollar. According to the museum experts, the head on the coin was "probably" the head of the Greek goddess Hera.

Thus, my childhood teacher who had originally enthralled me with the name, "Sextersius" had been wrong. The coin was not a "Sextersius"–*it was a "Semis."*

Decades after having found it, my search for my coin's identity was complete. I had treasured it, and protected it; yet, I had never stopped to consider how many hands it had touched over two thousand and two hundred years, and how many tragic events it had survived, all of those years. Now that its identity is clear, I can stop and reflect on its amazing history.

One day, about 2,200 years ago, someone in Hipponium had minted it; someone afterwards used it for the first time. What was bought with it that special day? It was probably given to a merchant, but what kind of merchant? Soon after, it was probably given to another customer who then went on to buy something else. The people who used it spoke Greek, and wore Greek clothing. The coin may have been in the hands of most of the people in Hipponium/Valentia, including the hands of some of the invading Roman soldiers.

How many children treasured it? How many delicious ancient treats did they buy with it? How many loaves of bread, fish and bread or cuts of meat did it help purchase?

The city of Hipponium went on to become a mostly Roman city for seven hundred years. It was invaded by barbarian tribes. It was under Byzantine control. The city was destroyed by the Saracens, and was left abandoned for two hundred years, until the Normans came along, and re-built it. And then the other conquests that followed, on the part of other European invaders.

When did the coin leave the city? Or was it simply lost centuries ago, and then found again by some lucky soul?

All that history is in my hands, every time I hold my beloved coin. And, as I ponder its amazing history, I feel richer for having found it, that boring Summer's day in Capistrano, and for now having it in my possession.

Thus the long search had ended. What followed was another search which was just as fascinating, and much more important: the search for my ancient roots.

Ancient Greek vases and figurines. Museo Archeologico Statale Vito Capalbi in Vibo Valentia.(M. Caputo)

Ancient Greek figurines. Museo Archeologico Statale Vito Capalbi in Vibo Valentia.(M. Caputo)

The Riace Bronzes: Two large, well-preserved 5th century B.C. Greek bronzes, found in the Mediterranean, in the province of Reggio Calabria. Museo Nazionale della Magna Grecia, in Reggio Calabria.(Me)

Museo Nazionale della Magna Grecia (Reggio Calabria). A vast collection of ancient Calabrian-Greek remains may be found in this very fine Calabrian museum. (Paverio Autellitano - Macarrones)

Archeologist, Cristiana La Serra. Picture taken during our visit to the Locri Epizefiri Museum in 2010. Cristiana has contributed significantly to the creation of this work, with personal knowledge, and invaluable scholarly material. (M. Caputo)

17. BACK TO CENTRAL GREECE

T he history of the arrival, and the growth of the Locrian colonies was now clear. The Locrians had come from Central Greece from a state named, "Lokris." The state was located on the northern side of the Corinthian Gulf, just north of the Peloponnesus. It was divided into two sections, divided by a mountain chain, the highest peak being Mount Parnassus.

Historians tend to disagree as to which Locrians came to Calabria. Some insist that they were the "Ozolian" Locrians from the South West; others hold the view that they were "Opuntian" Locrians from the city of Opus in the North East. Dr. Giuseppe Greco shared with me his certainty that they were "Ozolians," mainly from the city of Amphissa, just north of the Corinthian Gulf.

This disagreement goes all the way back to ancient times. Strabo, the ancient geographer, wrote with certainty that the Locrians who founded Locri Epizephyrii, in Calabria, were Ozolian colonizers.[clvii] On the contrary, Ephorus, another Greek historian, believed that the colonizers were Opuntian, from the city of Opus.[clviii]

Another disagreement revolves around the colonizers' social origins. Aristotle and Polibius agree with the view that the first group of colonizers were wealthy women who left their area of origins with their handsome, and probably younger servants, while their husbands were involved in far away wars.[clix]

This is disputed by Timeus, a Locrian philosopher, who labeled the first history as simply Athenian's attempt to discredit Locri, being a traditional ally of Sparta, Athen's enemy. His view was that, on the contrary, the original colonizers were members of the one hundred most noble families in Locrian Greece.[clx]   It is quite possible that both perspectives may have hold some truth, and that the colonizers came from both areas of Locris, and that they may have been both nobles and servants. One thing is for sure: the Greeks who founded Locri Epizephyrii were Locrians from Central Greece, and on that there is *total* agreement.

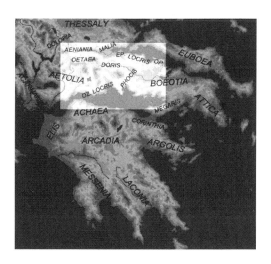

The ancient Greek states of Locris and Phocis in Central Greece.
My Greek ancestors moved to eastern Calabria from this area.
(William R. Shepher Historical Atlas)

18. SEARCHING FOR CRISSA

Historical sources are in total agreement as to who founded Locri Epizephyrii. They are also in agreement that it was these same people who founded Hipponion, in my area. What remained nebulous was who founded Crissa where the people in my area originated from. Was it the Locrians, the Phocians, who lived next to them in Central Greece, and who were of the same ethnic stock, or was it both? This problem was, in time, made more challenging, by the fact that some modern historians do not accept the evidence supporting the ancient view that there was a city named Crissa in Central Calabria, to begin with.

A thorough search made it clear that the sources attesting to the existence of an ancient city on the coast of Central Calabria named Crissa was based on the following sources:

1. The ancient Calabrian-Greek, tragic poet, Lycophron (285-247 B.C.), who wrote the poetic work, *Alexandra*, or *Cassandra*. In this ancient work, one finds the following reference, as quoted in Doctor Greco's book on the History of Rocca Angitola:

"The descendents of Naubulus will reach Temesa, where the Lampete, harsh promontory of the mountains of Hipponion, inclines toward the sea and before the Crissa Mountain will till the land."[clxi]

152

According to this translation, this is clearly a description of the area where Crissa is believed to have been founded, and it supports the perspective that a location named Crissa existed in Lycophon's days, in central Calabria, near the Angitola area.

2. We are also informed by Isacius, a Byzantine scholar who lived around the year 1070, that the Calabrian Crissa was a city of the Phocians, founded by Crissus (brother of Panopeus), upon his return from the Trojan War, in 1184 B.C. Crissus originated from Phocis a region of Greece and was the commander of the Phocian forces in Troy. Later, when the war ended, he departed to return home but, pushed by contrary winds, arrived, together with his companions, at the mouth of the Angitola River where attracted by the defensive potential of the hill nearby, founded the city named Crissa, after his own name.

Though enthralling, this story is seen by historians as nothing more than a myth. In fact, Dr. Giuseppe Greco is also convinced that it is no more than a legend, and that a more probable explanation is that the Phocians, who had helped found Locri Epizephyrii, most probably came from the eastern side of Calabria to the western side and founded Crissa.

> Its foundation (Crissa) goes back to the second half of the VII century B.C. when the Greeks from the Ionian side (of Calabria) moved to the Tyrrhenian side searching for new lands to colonize. A group of them, probably, Phocians who departed from Locri Epizephyrii with

whom they had been co-founders, stopped by the Angitola (river) and attracted by the fertility of the land and by the strategic position of the area, also on the hill covered today by ancient remains, founded the city that was given the name Crissa, from Crissa, city of the Phocians, in Greece.[clxii]

3. Gabriele Barrio, a well-known Calabrian historian who lived in the 1500's also shared the view that Crissa was founded by the Phocians. His views may have been based on Lycophron or, perhaps, other ancient sources we no longer have. He also believed that it was founded by the Greek hero, Crissus, as did Isacius.

4. Other sources which mention Crissa as the original city on the mountain by the Angitola River are the well-known ancient Calabrian historians, Fiore and Marafioti.[clxiii] They, too, held the same view that Crissus was the founder.

5. Dr. Greco shared with me that his grandfather told Dr. Greco's father that there was a tradition in Maierato, the town nearest to Rocca Angitola, that in the 1700's one could find a stone slab in the Rocca Fortress which stated, "Ic fuit Crissa" (Here was Crissa).

6. Gian Giacomo Martini, Catholic priest, and writer from San Nicola da Crissa, a town near mine. He mentions in his book, *Consiliorum Sive Responsorum Jure,* written in 1635, that Crissa was his ancient "Fatherland;" the land of his ancient ancestors, of

which he asserts to have seen superb ruins and tombstones.

Unfortunately, according to Martini, the Crissa he referred to was not located where the Rocca Angitola is today, but in a location he named, "Le Motte." We have no way of knowing where this location was. Perhaps it was located in the Scrisi Plain, in the Rocca area, but only time, and archaeological excavations will tell.

7. The fact that the plain adjacent to the Rocca Angitola is called, "La Piana degli Scrisi," (The Scrisi Plain or the Plain of the Scrisans) may also have significance. The Scrisans may very well have been "Crissans" in ancient time, that is the people who anciently occupied the area.

Thus, according to this perspective, the Phocians created two colonies just north of Hipponion, one named Napitia, in the area of Pizzo Calabro of today, and one just north of Napitia, on the mountain next to the Angitola River, which they named after their city of origin: Crissa, around the second half of the VII century B.C.

The hill the city was located on overlooked the Gulf of St. Eufemia. It was a stunning location, somewhat reminiscent of the gulf near the city of Crissa, back in Greece, but probably more scenic, given its high location.

Unfortunately, as time went on, it became clear that this perspective was not unchallenged. Initially, I had read some criticisms of the above perspective, but I had found them quite superficial and unsupported.

When, in Summer of 2010, I visited my friend and relative, Pino La Serra, in Vibo Valentia, I finally had the opportunity to discuss the issue with his archeologist daughter, Cristiana, who informed me that, in fact, Lycophron's above-mentioned verses from his *Alexandra* had been translated incorrectly by some ancient and some modern scholars. The translation she favored was the following:

In Temesa will arrive the mariners

Of the descendents of Naubulus, there were the harsh

Horn of the Mountain of Hipponion juts out to sea

Of Lampetia and "instead" of the land of Crisa

They will work the land with a ploughshare pulled by oxen

The land of Croton on the isthmus

Regretting their native Lilea, the plains

Of Anomorea, Anphissa, and the illustrious Abe.[clxiv]

Clearly, this translation emphasizes that the Greek newcomers to the area had come from the region where Locris borders Phocis, in Greece, where Crissa and the other well-known cities were located. The passage also emphasizes that those people missed their homeland. It does not in any way refer to any city in Calabria named Crissa.

This alternative translation clearly muddled the waters, and added doubt to the critical and foundational proof that Crissa existed in my area.

Since both translations were seemingly possible, more research had to be done into the original wording of Lycophron's passage.

Further research, in fact, supported the fact that both translations were possible. Translators of the *Alexandra* such as, Fusillo[clxv] and Mair[clxvi] favor the latter translation. Two French editions, one by Hurst and Kolde[clxvii] and the Etude Grecque edition by Debaisieux,[clxviii] contrariwise, supported a translation similar to the one chosen by Giuseppe Greco, which supports the view that, indeed, there was a Crissa in my area.

Thus the use of Lycophron's *Alexandra* to support the existence of Crissa in my area clearly hangs in doubt. What Lycophron *does* support is the view that the ethnic group which found the Greek colony in my area originated in Phocis, which is also supported by all ancient Calabrian historians, and a number of recent ones, including Greco.

Yet, with great probability, the story of Crissus is one more mythical story created by ancient people to give their colonies a glorious origin. The most common way of accomplishing this task was to associate the origin of Greek colonies to a hero who, after leaving Troy, had lost his way and pushed by the winds ended up in the area where the new colony was founded.

Thus the *specific* origin of the people who settled in my area is in doubt. What is not in doubt is the fact that they were Greeks who had left the northern side of the Peloponnesus. They were of the ethnic group which included both the Locrians and the Phocians. Thus, whether they were Locrians, Phocians, or both, they were essentially the same people.

19. MORE ABOUT THE PHOCIANS

Like the Locrians, the Phocians inhabited the central part of Greece, north of the Corinthian Gulf, bordered by Mount Parnassus, and the Locrian Mountains, on the north. Between the two mountain ranges, in the Cephissis River Valley, were found most of the Phocian settlements: Amphicleia (or Amphicaea), Tithorea, Elatea, Hyampolis, Abae, and Daulis. A mountain spur projecting south from Mount Parnassus towards the gulf separated the city of Krisa (Crissa) and its port, Cyrrha, on the Crisaean plain.

Its early history is hard to decipher. Phocis was mainly pastoral, and the population was thought to be descendents of the Aeolians, one of the oldest Greek-speaking peoples in the area.

The Phocians controlled the famed sanctuary of Delphi, and benefited greatly from the tolls, and the gifts left in the area by the pilgrims. In 590 B.C., the Crissan Phocians became greedy, and started charging unacceptably high tolls on the pilgrims at Cyrrha, on their way to Delphi. A coalition of Greek states declared a sacred war, destroyed Crissa, and transferred the sanctuary to the control of a council representing neighboring communities.[clxix] The view that the Calabrian Crissa may have been populated by Crissans from the Greek Crissa may have some substance, due to the fact that it was next door to Amphissa, a major Locrian city that, without doubt, would have contributed to the growth of Locri Epizephyrii. Some of Crissa's inhabitants may have joined their neighbors, and may have followed them to their America. During the sacred war, and especially after their defeat, it may be conceivable that some, or many, may have found safety in Locri Epizephyrii, as well.

Amphissa, Greece, today. Some, or most of the Greek ancestors of the people of the Angitola Valley may have emigrated to Calabria from this general area. The dry, rocky land in the background would explain the need to move to a less challenging location. (Alaniaris)

Mount Parnassus: A mount in the area of Greece where both the Locrians and the Phocians lived. The famed city of Delphi is located in this area. (Electron08)

Delphi: Greek Amphitheatre. (Kolossus)

WHO WERE MY ANCIENT ANCESTORS, THEN?

Let us now summarize where we stand. It is absolutely certain that the ancient people who colonized the coastal areas where my ancestors originated from were Greeks. There might have been a first wave of Phocians, which began the colonization, but it was for certain followed by a second *major* wave of Locrians, who came from Locri Epizephyrii.

Given the Phocians' ethnic affinity to Locrians, and the close proximity of some of their major cities to major Locrian cities, such as Amphissa, some may very well have taken the opportunity to follow their neighbors to Calabria, their new Promised Land, and may have settled there with them.

The ancient indigenous peoples which the newcomers displaced, moved inland. Where did they end up over time? Hard to know. Did some, in time, blend in with the Greek population? Some might have.

The Bruzi, from Central Italy, came down and conquered all the Greek colonies, and controlled them for decades. Was there some mixing with them? There appears to have been a fair amount of mixing in Northern Calabria, but much less so in Central and Southern Calabria. Dr. Giuseppe Greco's view is that the people of the Angitola Valley *did not* mix with the Bruzi.

The Latins came down, conquered all of Calabria, and ruled it for about 700 years. Many Central Italians came down to populate the new Roman colonies. They, without doubt, intermarried with the local Greeks, over the centuries. This may have been more common in large centers such as Hipponium and other coastal communities, and much less so in smaller communities away from major centers and, especially, away from the coast. Again, Dr. Greco is of the view that though our ancient Greek ancestors did mix with the Latins, they remained "mostly" Greek. How much so? It is impossible to know.

During the Byzantine period there was a significant influx of new, Greek-speaking peoples, which may have further strengthened the Greek genetic component of my people. How many of them moved to my area? Hard to know. It is conceivable that some may have followed the Basilian priests to the various areas where they founded convents. Two such convents were founded in my area.

Of course, for the past 1000 years there has been a constant *trickle* of people from other parts of Italy into Calabria, and a tiny few from other occupying countries, such as the Arabs, the Nordic Normans, and the Spanish who, during their invasions, may have blended in with the local population. Given the fact that my area was not easily accessible, and that it was not as prosperous as other parts of Italy, we can surmise that the "trickle" may have been very small indeed, thus leaving the ancient Greek, and Latin genetic components to continue predominating.

CONCLUSION

O ver one year has gone by, since I started writing this book. It has been an amazing adventure with both exciting and sobering discoveries. I have learned much about my people's history, and, in so doing, I have been saddened to discover that they have been shaped by the crucible of wars, invasions, disastrous earthquakes, hunger and disease.

It is quite probable that the proverbial stubbornness, and forcefulness of Calabrians has some genetic root. After all, our ancestors were predominantly two fearsome people: the unstoppable ancient Romans, and the quarrelsome ancient Greeks (in Northern Calabria, add the fierce Brutii). A blend of these peoples cannot but produce a forceful temperament–and that many Calabrians definitely have.

But the character of a people is also shaped by their history. Besides being stubborn and forceful, many Calabrians also tend to be cynical about life, and suspicious of human motives. Many also tend to be negativistic about the future, and critical about the present.

My search has made clear to me the reasons for my people's negativistic, fatalistic and suspicious mental set. It has to do with millennia of suffering, of terror, of unpredictable and unstoppable destructive events; of having to be weary of others' motives, given the intense competition over scarce resources and, most of all, the gnawing, chronic anxiety that the unexpected–earthquakes, floods, landslides, disease, etc.–can wipe out their possessions, or their loved ones, within a very short period of time.

My increased awareness of what dwells within the psyche of my people has also greatly increased my respect, and my love for them. They are a people shaped with the mortar of suffering and, yet, they continue bearing their daily struggles with much patience, always hoping that life might, if nothing else, afford them some reprieve.

These are my people–and they are me. I share their weaknesses–but I also share their strengths. And now, more than ever, I am very glad to be the descendent of the strong, courageous, and resilient people of that special, and beautiful land called, Calabria.

ABOUT THE AUTHOR

MICHAEL CAPUTO was born in the beautiful Region of Calabria, in Southern Italy, but has resided in Canada most of his life, with intervals in both Los Angeles and Rome, Italy. Michael holds a BA in Psychology, a Bachelor of Education, a Masters' Degree in Psychology and Education, and several teaching qualifications. Michael taught, and counseled at the high school level for over two decades, while teaching part time at the college level for sixteen years. Michael is the author of the award-winning book, *God Seen Through the Eyes of the Greatest Minds.* He is married to Leonilda, and is the proud father of three special children: Anthony, Julie and Victor.

WORKS CITED

ⁱ Renoir, Jean. *Renoir, My Father*. Toronto: Little, Brown and Company, 1962. 234. Print.

ⁱⁱ Renoir 234.

ⁱⁱⁱ Renoir 235.

^{iv} Renoir 235.

^v Renoir 235.

^{vi} Renoir 236.

^{vii} Renoir 236.

^{viii} Renoir 236.

^{ix} Renoir 236.

^x La Serra, Pino. "Percorso della memoria: il ricordo del pittore Pierre Auguste Renoir." *Capistrano and its Children*. n.d. n. page. Web. 21 July 2012. <http://www.capistranocalabria.com/renoirpresentation.htm>.

^{xi} Fera, Andrea. *Renoir in Calabria. Prodotto di un'inchiesta*. Patti (ME), Italy: Casa Editrice Kimerik, 2012. Web. <http://www.bookville.it/Utente/Books/BookDetail.aspx?ISBN=97888 60967459>.

^{xii} Andrea is the son of Brunina, "The Gracious young lady" mentioned on page 30, who later married another dear friend, Lino Fera.

^{xiii} "The 1908 Messina Earthquake: 100-Year Retrospective." *Risk Management Solutions*. 2008. 2. Web. 21 July 2012. <http://www.rms.com/publications/1908_messina_earthquake.pdf>.

^{xiv} Squillaci, Michele, et al. "I grandi disastri in Italia." *www.cronologia.leonardo.it*. 2012. n. page. Web. 15 July 2012. <http://cronologia.leonardo.it/storia/a1905c.htm>.

^{xv} "Il terremoto in Calabria 1905." *sempre in penombra*. 11 April 2009. n. page. Web. 15 July 2012. <http://sempreinpenombra.com/2009/04/11/il-terremoto-in-calabria-1905/>.

[xvi] M. Quasimodo, *Terremoto e soccorsi in Calabria: Breve relazione dei fatti di Calabria.* Napoli: Tipografia Vitale, 1905. Ristampa Walter Brenner, Cosenza, 1991, 7–9. In, Bagnato, Antonio. "Appunti sul terremoto del 1905 nel vibonese." *Incontri mediterranei.* 2005. n. page. Web. 15 July 2012. <http://www.impressionisoggettive.it/terr appunti sul terremoto 1905.htm>.

[xvii] Manduca, Nello. *Arsura.* Chieri: Tipografia Ghirardi, 1978. 157. Print.

[xviii] Quasimodo 7-9.

[xix] Quasimodo 7-9.

[xx] American Geographical Society of New York. *Bulletin of the American Geographical Society, Volume 4, Volumes 712-716 of American Periodical Series, 1850-1900.* American Geographical Society of New York, 1909. 414. Google Books. Web. 22 May 2013.

[xxi] "Il rischio sismico in Calabria." *Protezione Civile della Calabria.* 2 12 2011: n. page. Web. 05 06 2013. <http://www.protezionecivilecalabria.it/index.php?option=com_content&view=article&id=85:il-rischio-sismico-in-calabria&catid=45:sismicco&Itemid=65>.

[xxii] Vivenzio, Giovanni. *Istoria de' tremuoti avvenuti nella provincia della Calabria ulteriore e nella città de Messina nell' anno 1783: e di quanto nella Calabria fu fatto per lo suo risorgimento fino al 1787: preceduta da una teoria, ed istoria generale de' tremuoti.* Napoli: Stamperia Regale, 1788. 171. Google Books. Web. 22 May 2013.

[xxiii] Manfrida, Giovanni. *Capistrano ieri ed oggi.* Soveria Mannelli (CZ): Calabria Letteraria Editrice, 1987, 46.

[xxiv] Rumiz, Paolo. "L'anno zero della Calabria." *Bagnara Calabra.* 11 8 2009: n. page. Web. 15 July 2012. <http://bagnararc.it/news_09/09_08_11.html>.

[xxv] Jacques, E., et al. "Faulting and Earthquake Triggering During the 1783 Calabria Seismic Sequence." *Geophys. J. Int.* 147. (2001): 503. n.d. Web. 15 July 2012. <http://www.geologie.ens.fr/~vigny/articles/calabre_1783.pdf>.

[xxvi] Tagarelli, Antonio. "Il Terremoto del 1783 e la Malaria." *Bagnara Calabra.* n.d. n. page. Web. 15 July 2012. <http://www.bagnararc.it/cultura/terremoto1783_malaria.html>.

[xxvii] The biblical name given to Filadelfia was proposed by Bishop Serrao "...so that the inhabitants would remember their Greek origins, so as to remember and imitate the virtues of their ancestors and above all so that they would love each other as brothers and friends, having also the same sentiment toward all of humanity."

[xxviii] Colletta, Pietro. *Storia del Reame di Napoli.* Capolago, 1838. In, Pata, Franco. "Storia di Mileto: dall'età postnormanna al terremoto del 1783." *Sistema Bibliotecario Vibonese.* n.d. n. page. Web. 15 July 2012. <http://www.sbvibonese.vv.it/sezionec/pag240_c.asp&xgt;>.

[xxix] Colletta.

[xxx] Serrao, Elia. "I Tremuoti in Calabria." In Serrao, Gaspare. *Castel Monardo e Filadelfia nella loro storia.* Filadelfia: Tipografia Artigiana, 1983. 143-144. Print.

[xxxi] Serrao 145.

[xxxii] Cagliostro, Rosa, Maria. *1783-1796: la ricostruzione delle parrocchie nei disegni di Cassa Sacra: contributo alla storia dell'architettura del '700 in Calabria.* Soveria Mannelli, Calabria, Italy: Rubettino, 2000. Google Books. Web. 22 May 2013.

[xxxiii] D'Amato, V. "Memorie historiche di Catanzaro." In, Serrao, Gaspare. *Castel Monardo e Filadelfia nella loro storia.* Filadelfia: Tipografia Artigiana, 1983. 121. Print.

[xxxiv] Manfrida 46.

[xxxv] "Il Rischio Sismico in Calabria."

[xxxvi] Burke, Edmund. *Dodsley's Annual Register, or a View of the History, Politics, and Literature for the Year 1783.* London: J. Dodsley, 1785. 58. Google Books. Web. 22 May 2013.

[xxxvii] Townsend, George. *The Manual of Dates.* London: Frederick Warne, 1877. 334. Google Books. Web. 22 May 2013.

[xxxviii] Sale, George, et al. *The Modern Part of an Universal History, from the*

Earliest Accounts to the Present Time. 43. London: MDCCLXXX. 151. Google Books. Web. 22 May 2013.

[xxxix] Poggio, Pier Paolo. *Storia Sociale della Calabria.* Milano: Jacka Book, 1976. 18. Google Books. Web. 22 May 2013.

[xl] Galli, Paolo, Bosi, Vittorio. "Catastrophic 1638 Earthquakes in Calabria (Southern Italy): New Insights from Paleoseismological Investigation." *Journal of Geophysical Research.* 108.NO. B1 (2004): 5. n.d. Web. 15 July 2012. <http://www. iesn.org/dida/sila.pdf>.

[xli] Kircher, Athanasius. "Earthquake at Calabria in the Year 1638." In, Johonnot, James. *Geographical Reader.* Stanford: Stanford University Libraries, 1888. 41-45. Google Books. Web. 22 May 2013.

[xlii] Serrao 119.

[xliii] Teti, Vito. "Il terremoto del 1908 in Calabria in una trama di abbandoni di lunga durata." In, Bertolaso, G., et al. *Il terremoto e il maremoto del 28 dicembre 1908: analisi sismologica, impatto, prospettive.* Roma–Bologna: DPC–INGV, 2008, 813.

[xliv] Gregory, Desmond, *Napoleon's Italy.* Cranberry, New Jersey: Associated University Presses, 2001. 171. Google Books. Web. 22 May 2013.

[xlv] Desmond 171.

[xlvi] "The Napoleon Correspondence." *Edinburgh Review or Critical Journal.* 126. (1867): 341. Google Books. Web. 22 May, 2013.

[xlvii] Ferrari, Giuseppe. *L'insurrezione calabrese nel 1806 e l'assedio di Amantea.* Officina Poligrafica, 1911. 92. Google Books. Web. 22 May 2013.

Ilari, Virgilio. *Le Due Sicilie nelle guerre napoleoniche: 1800-1815.* Stato maggiore dell'esercito, ufficio storico, 2008. 509. Google Books. Web. 22 May 2013.

[xlviii] Brosacchio, G. *Storia economica della Calabria.* Chiaravalle Centrale, Calabria, Italy: Effe emme, 1980. In, Manfrida, *Capistrano* 91.

[xlix] Littel, Eliakim. *Living Age.* Boston: Little and Gay, 1867. 537. Google Books. Web. 3 June 2013.

[l] Manfrida 20-21

[li]Tripodi, A. *L'ultimo decennio di Rocca Angitola,* in «Calabria Letteraria», XXXV. 1987. 7-9. Tripodi, A. *Calabria tra Cinquecento e Ottocento.* Ricerche d'archivio. Reggio Calabria: Jason Editrice, 1994. In, Teti, Vito, *Il Senso dei Luoghi.* Roma: Donzelli Editore, 2004. 173. Google Books. Web. 22 May 2013.

[lii] La Serra, Cristiana. "Abitati medievali nella Valle dell'Angitola." Diss. University of Pisa. 20.

[liii] La Serra 173.

[liv] Greco, Giuseppe. *Rocca Angitola, nella storia e nella leggenda.* Vibo Valentia, Italy: Mapograf, 1985. 75. Print.

[lv] Greco, *Rocca Angitola* 75.

[lvi] Martire, manuscript II, 406, V. In, La Serra 20.

[lvii] Marafioti, Girolamo. *Croniche et antichita` di Calabria.* Napoli: Stamperia dello Stigliola, 1595, 212-213. In, Greco, *Rocca Angitola* 65.

[lviii] Greco, *Rocca Angitola* 75.

[lix] D'Orsi, Lutio. *I terremoti delle due Calavrie.* Cited in, Neapoli Typis Roberti Molli, 1640. In, Greco, *Rocca Angitola* 69.

[lx] Greco, *Rocca Angitola* 70.

[lxi] Barrio, Gabriele. *De antiquitate et situ Calabriae.* Roma: Ex Typographia S. Michaelis ad Ripam Sumtibus Hieronimi Mainardi, 1737. 129. In, Greco, *Rocca Angitola* 64.

[lxii] Greco, *Rocca Angitola* 65.

[lxiii] Greco, *Rocca Angitola* 66.

[lxiv] La Serra 19

[lxv] Greco, *Rocca Angitola* 58.

[lxvi] Greco, *Rocca Angitola* 60.

[lxvii] Greco, *Rocca Angitola* 60.

Michael Caputo

[lxviii] Greco, *Rocca Angitola* 60.

[lxix] Giustiniani, Lorenzo. *Dizionario geografico*, Tomo, VIII, 20. In, Greco, *Rocca Angitola* 6.

[lxx] Greco, *Rocca Angitola* 51.

[lxxi] Greco, *Rocca Angitola* 53.

[lxxii] La Serra 18.

[lxxiii] La Serra 18.

[lxxiv] Accademia Pontaniana. *I registri della cancelleria Angioina*, 18, Vol. XXXIV. In, La Serra 18.

[lxxv] *I Registri della Cancelleria Angioina*, 68. In, La Serra 18.

[lxxvi] Accademia Pontaniana, *Fonti Aragonesi*, Vol. I, 5-7. In, La Serra 18.

[lxxvii] Greco, *Rocca Angitola* 47.

[lxxviii] Greco, *Rocca Angitola* 47.

[lxxix] Greco, *Rocca Angitola* 44.

[lxxx] *I Registri della Cancelleria Angioina*, vol. XIII. Napoli, 1954. 28. In, Greco, *Rocca Angitola* 45.

[lxxxi] Pardi, Giuseppe. *I Registri Angioini e la popolazione calabrese*, ASPN. Cited in, Luigi Lubano, Napoli, 1921. 36-45. In, Greco, *Rocca Angitola* 45.

[lxxxii] Greco, *Rocca Angitola* 46.

[lxxxiii] Winkelmann, Eduard. *Acta Imperii Inedita*. Innsbruck: Wagner'schen Universitats-Buchhandlung, 1880. 82-83. In, Greco, *Rocca Angitola* 42.

[lxxxiv] Neveaux, Francois. *A Brief History of the Normans*. London: Constable & Robinson Ltd., 2008, 159.

[lxxxv] Neveaux 159

[lxxxvi] Malaterra, Goffredo. De Rebus gestis Rogerii et Roberti Guiscardi, I, XX. In, Greco, *Rocca Angitola* 39.

[lxxxvii] Greco, *Rocca Angitola* 40.

[lxxxviii] Greco, *Rocca Angitola* 40.

[lxxxix] Greco, *Rocca Angitola* 40.

[xc] Greco, Giuseppe. "Rocca Angitola, Rocca Niceforo, Crissa. " *Pro Loco. Rocca Angitola.* n.d. n. page. Web. 4 April 2010. <http://www.prolocomaierato.net/rocca-angitola-rocca-niceforo-crissa.html>.

[xci] Manfrida 37.

[xcii] Manfrida 43.

[xciii] Manfrida 37.

[xciv] Manfrida 38

[xcv] "Ducato di Calabria." *Wikipedia.* n.d. n. page. Web. 16 July 2012. <http://it.wikipedia.org/wiki/Ducato_di_Calabria>.

[xcvi] Sinopoli, Cesare, et al. *La Calabria: storia, geografia, arte.* Soveria Mannelli, Italy: Rubettino, 2004. 29. Google Books. Web. 22 May 2013.

[xcvii] Sinopoli et al. 29.

[xcviii] Placanica, Augusto. *Storia della Calabria, dall'antichita` ai nostri giorni.* Roma: Donzelli Editore, 1993. 75. Google Books. Web. 22 May 2013.

[xcix] Martorana, Carmelo. *Notizie storiche dei Saraceni Siciliani.* Palermo: Pedoni e Muratori, 1832. 128. Google Books. Web. 22 May 2013.

[c] La Serra 25.

[ci] Serrao, Gaspare. *Castel Monardo e Filadelfia nella loro storia.* Filadelfia, Italy: Tipografia Artigiana, 1783.194. Print.

[cii] Serrao 197.

[ciii] Greco, *Rocca Angitola* 30.

[civ] Greco, *Rocca Angitola* 29.

[cv] Greco, *Rocca Angitola* 30.

[cvi] Greco, *Rocca Angitola, Rocca Niceforo, Crissa.*

[cvii] Greco, *Rocca Angitola, Rocca Niceforo, Crissa.*

[cviii] Hansen, M. H., Nielsen, T.H. *An Inventory of Archaic and Classical Poleis.* Oxford: Oxford University Press, 2004. 282.

Cox, George W. *History of Greece.* London: C. Kegan Paul and Co., 1878. 152. Google Books. Web. 22 May 2013.

[cix] Cerchiai, Luca, et al. *Citta` Greche della Magna Grecia e della Sicilia.* Verona: Arsenale Editrice, 2001. 92. Print.

[cx] D'Andrea, Maria, Floriani, Gilberto. "Hipponium - Valentia: dalla poleis al municipium."*Sistema Bibliotecario Vibonese.* n.d. n. page. Web. 17 July 2012.<http://www.sbvibonese.vv.it/sezionec/pag209_c.asp&xgt;>.

[cxi] Luke the Evangelist. "The Book of Acts." *The Holy Bible.* NKJV. New York: Thomas Nelson, 1983. 28:13. Print.

[cxii]"History of the Jews in Calabria." *Wikipedia.* n.d.n. page Web. 17 July 2012. <http://en.wikipedia.org/wiki/History_of_the_Jews_in_Calabria>.

[cxiii] Gianolio, Emanuele. "Gli ebrei a Trani e in Puglia nel medioevo." Diss. Universita` degli studi di Bari. Web. 17 July 2012. <http://www.morasha.it/tesi/gnlo/gnlo01.html>.

[cxiv] Primack, Karen. "Rabbi Aiello Making a Difference in Italy's South." *Kulanu-All of Us.* 2008: n. page. Web. 17 July 2012. <http://www.kulanu.org/italy/aiellosouthitaly.php>.

[cxv] Cerchiai. *Citta` Greche della Magna Grecia e della Sicilia.* 7.

[cxvi] Magna Grecia."*Questia Encyclopedia.* n.d. n. page. Web. 17 July 2012. <http://www.questia.com/library/encyclopedia/magna-graecia.jsp>.

[cxvii] "Timeo." *LocriAntica.it.* n.d. n. page. Web. 17 July 2012. <http://www.locriantica.it/personaggi/altri_personaggi.htm>.

[cxviii] Scrivo, Adriano. "Pitagora." *Kaulon.it.* n.d. n. page. Web. 17 July 2012.

<http://www.kaulon.it/pitagora.htm>.

[cxix] Crane, G. R. (Editor). "Milo of Kroton." *Perseus Digital Library*. n.d. n. page. Web. 17 July 2012. <http://www.perseus.tufts.edu/Olympics/milo.html>.

[cxx] Lahanas, Michael. "Famous Ancient Greek Athletes." *Hellenica*. n.d. n. page. Web. 17 July 2012. <http://www.mlahanas.de/Greeks/Athletes.htm>.

[cxxi] Barone, Vincenzo. "La Calabria: Il Nome." *Calabria*. n.d. n. page. Web. 17 July 2012. <http://www.calabria.nu/nome.htm>.

[cxxii] "Italy." *AllWords.com*. n.d. n. page. Web. 17 July 2012. <http://www.allwords.com/word-Italy.html>.

[cxxiii] Fabio, Michelle. "History of Calabria." *Bleeding Espresso*. n.d. n. page. Web. 17 July 2012. <http://bleedingespresso.com/calabria/history-of-calabria>.

[cxxiv] "La colonizzazione e il periodo Greco." *Locri Antica*. n.d. n. page. Web. 17 July 2012. <http://www.locriantica.it/storia/per_greco1.htm>.

[cxxv] "Siculi." *Encyclopædia Britannica. Encyclopædia Britannica Online*. Encyclopædia Britannica Inc., 2012. Web. 17 July 2012 <http://www.britannica.com/EBchecked/topic/542900/Siculi>.

[cxxvi] "Locri." *In Italy Today*. n.d. n. page. Web. 17 July 2012. <http://www.initalytoday.com/calabria/locri/index.htm>.

[cxxvii] "La colonizzazione e l'origine dei coloni." *Locri Antica*. n.d. n. page. Web. 17 July 2012. <http://www.locriantica.it/storia/per_greco1.htm>.

[cxxviii] "Collocazione geografica."*Locri Antica*. n.d. n. page. Web. 17 July 2012. <http://www.locriantica.it/geografia.htm>.

[cxxix] Strabo. *Geografia*. VI, 7. In, Locri Antica. n.d. n. page. Web. 17 July 2012. <http://www.locriantica.it/geografia.htm>.

[cxxx] "Milo of Croton."*Encyclopædia Britannica. Encyclopædia Britannica Online*. Encyclopædia Britannica Inc., 2012. n.d. n. page. Web. 17 July 2012 <http://www.britannica.com/EBchecked/topic/383062/Milo-of-Croton>.

cxxxi "Rhegium (Rhegion). "*Hellenica*. Web. 17 July 2012.
<http://www.mlahanas.de/Greeks/Cities/Rhegium.html >.

cxxxii "Campaign at Monte Palazzi, a Mountain Fort of Locri Epizephyrii."
Foundation for Calabrian Archaeology. 30 March 2011. Web. 17 July
2012. <http://digcalabria.org.p2.hostingprod.com/news>.

"La Fondazione di Hipponion." *ArcheoCalabriaVirtual, Soprintendenza per i
Beni Archeologici della Calabria*. 2007. n. page. Web. 17 July 2012.
<http://www.archeocalabria.beniculturali.it/archeovirtualtour/calabriaw
eb/hipponio1.htm>.

cxxxiv Lampriere, John. *A Classical Dictionary*. 5th. New York: Evert Duyckinck,
George Long, W. H. Gilley, Collins and Co., and Collins and Hanney,
1825. Google Books. Web. 22 May, 2013.

"Battle of the Sagra" *The Full Wiki*. Web. 17 July 2012.
<http://www.thefullwiki.org/Battle_of_the_Sagra>.

cxxxv Erasmus, Desiderius. *Collected Works of Erasmus: Literary and
Educational Writings*. 24. Toronto: University of Toronto Press, 1978.
447. Google Books. Web. 22 May 2013.

cxxxvi Redfield, J. M. *The Locrian Maidens: Love and Death in Greek Italy*.
Princeton, NJ: Princeton University Press, 2003. 252. Google Books.
Web. 22 May 2013.

cxxxvii The Full Wiki, *"The Battle of the Sagra."*

cxxxviii Mogens, H. H., Nielsen, T.L. *An Inventory of Archaic and Classical
Poleis*. Oxford: University Press, 2004. 291. Google Books. Web. 22
May 2013.

cxxxix Zappala, Natale. "La battaglia della Sagra." *CatanzaroNotizie.it*. 29 12
2009: n.d.n. page. Web. 17 Jul. 2012.
<http://www.catanzaronotizie.it/200912289729/la-battaglia-della-
sagra.html>.

"Il VI secolo e lo scontro con Crotone." *Locri Antica*. n.d. n. page. Web. 17 July
2012. <http://www.locriantica.it/storia/per_greco3.htm>.

[cxl] "Il VI secolo e lo scontro con Crotone." *Locri Antica.*

[cxli] Wheeler, Graham. "Battlefield Epiphanies in Ancient Greece: A Survey." *Digressus: The Internet Journal of the Classical World.* 4. (2004): 1. Web. 17 July 2012. <http://www.digressus.org/articles/2004pp01-14-art-wheeler.pdf>.

[cxlii] "Il VI secolo e lo scontro con Crotone." *Locri Antica.*

[cxliii] "Dioskouroi Cult." *Theoi Greek Mythology.* n.d. n. page. Web. 17 July 2012. <http://www.theoi.com/Cult/DioskouroiCult.html>.

[cxliv] Niebuhr, B.G. *Lectures on Ancient History, from the Earliest Times to the Taking of Alexandria by Octavianus* . 3. Philadelphia: Blanchard and Lea, 1852. 211. Google Books. Web. 22 May 2013.

[cxlv] "Il VI secolo e lo scontro con Crotone." *Locri Antica.*

[cxlvi] Redfield, *The Locrian Maidens: Love and Death in Greek Italy,* 254.

[cxlvii] "Sybaris." *Questia.* n.d. n. page. Web. 17 July 2012. <http://www.questia.com/library/encyclopedia/sybaris.jsp>.

"Sparta's Menelaus-Al Symptoms, or the Plot Sickens."*tribwatch.com.* Feb. 2007. n. page. Web. 17 July 2012. <http://www.tribwatch.com/locrian.htm>.

"Croton." *statemaster.com.* Web. 17 July 2012. <http://www.statemaster.com/encyclopedia/Croton>.

[cxlviii] Shuré, Eduard. *Pythagoras and the Delphic Mysteries.* 1906. 169. Web. <http://www.sacred-texts.com/cla/pdm/pdm06.htm>.

[cxlix] Boardman, John, Hammond N.G.L. *The Cambridge Ancient History: The Expansion of the Greek World, 8th to 6th Centuries B.C.* Cambridge: University Press, 2002. 195. Google Books. Web. 22 May 2013.

[cl] Redfield, *The Locrian Maidens: Love and Death in Greek Italy* 205.

[cli] Redfield 205.

[clii] Redfield 205.

cliii Redfield 205.

cliv "La Fondazione di Hipponion." *ArcheoCalabriaVirtual.*

clv "La storia di Vibo Valentia." *pavonerisorse.it.* n.d. n. page. Web. 17 July
    2012. <http://www.pavonerisorse.it/cacrt/intbim/vibohome.html>.

clvi Accardo, Simona. *Villae Romanae nell&Ager Bruttius.* Roma: "L'erma" do
    Bretschnaider, 2000. 27. Google Books. Web. 22 May 2013.

clvii "Locrians." *Academic Dictionaries and Encyclopedias.* Web. 17 July 2012.
    <http://en.academic.ru/dic.nsf/enwiki/4014385>.

clviii "La Colonizzazione e le Origini dei Coloni." *Locri Antica.* n.d. n. page.
    Web. 17 July 2012. <http://www.locriantica.it/storia/per_greco1.htm>.

clix Cerchiai, Luca, et al. *Citta` Greche della Magna Grecia e della Sicilia* 90.

clx "La Colonizzazione e le Origini dei Coloni." *Locri Antica.*

clxi Greco, *Rocca Angitola, nella storia e nella leggenda* 13.

clxii Greco, *Rocca Angitola, nella storia e nella leggenda* 14.

clxiii Galloro, Antonio. "Profilo storico di San Nicola da Crissa (V.V.)."
    sscrocifisso.vv.it. July, 2005. n. page. Web. 17 July 2012.
    <http://www.sscrocifisso.vv.it/articoli2005/giornatemediche05/profilo_
    storico_di_san_nicola_da.htm>.

clxiv La Serra 21.

clxv Fusillo, Massimo, Hurst, André. *Lycophron, Alessandra.* Guerini e Associati,
    1991. 127. Google Books. Web. 22 May 2013.

clxvi Mair, A.W. (Translator). *Lycophron, Alexandra.* Web.
    <http://www.theoi.com/Text/LycophronAlexandra.html>.

clxvii Lycophron. *Alexandra.* Collection des universités de France: Série grecque,
    Vol. 468. (André Hurst: Editor, Antje Kolde, translator). Belles Lettres.
    2008. 38. Google Books. Web. 22 May, 2013.

clxviii Lycophron. *Alexandra.* (Chauvin, C., Cusset, C. translators). Paris:
    L'harmattan, 2008. 87. Google Books. Web. 22 May 2013.

clxix "Phocis." *Encyclopædia Britannica. Encyclopædia Britannica Online.* Encyclopædia Britannica Inc., n.d. n.page. Web. 17 July 2012. <http://www.britannica.com/EBchecked/topic/457077/Phocis>.

Made in the USA
Charleston, SC
16 June 2013